SPIRITUAL GIFTS
AND
THEIR OPERATION

Anecdotal Lectures
Delivered by
HOWARD CARTER

GOSPEL PUBLISHING HOUSE
Springfield, Missouri

02-0593

CONTENTS

Preface 3

1. The Gifts of the Spirit 5
2. The Word of Wisdom 16
3. The Word of Knowledge 27
4. Faith 37
5. Gifts of Healing 48
6. The Working of Miracles 60
7. Prophecy 70
8. Discerning of Spirits 76
9. Tongues and Interpretations 84

© Copyright, 1968
by the Gospel Publishing House
Springfield, Missouri 65802
5th Printing 1988
ISBN 0-88243-593-0

PRINTED IN U·S·A

PREFACE

The subject of spiritual gifts has been of great interest to the writer since the early days of the first World War and has continued to absorb his thoughts and attention over the years. The studies in this book were taken down stenographically from lectures delivered in New Zealand in his Auckland Church during his pastorate there of two years. After some necessary revision they are presented in this volume to satisfy those who have requested their publication.

The author's former book on the subject *Questions and Answers on the Gifts of the Spirit* differs considerably from this one, chiefly in that it deals with questions on the subject answered with the utmost brevity; whereas this book is concerned more with specific instances and stories that make for easy reading. It is hoped that pastors and students will appreciate the practical approach to the functioning of the gifts in the Church, and that other readers will find the simple personal narrative to their liking.

The division of the nine gifts into three groupings—Gifts of Revelation, Gifts of Power, and Gifts of Inspiration—was revealed to the writer shortly after commencing the study of the subject seriously. It has been a source of gratitude to God to find that most writers of today have been pleased to accept this classification, confirming that the light which came in the early days when there were no books available on the subject was from the Lord. Some who have written on the subject of the gifts have later revised what they wrote at first, and later still, have further revised their teaching. We cannot help but feel that when light comes directly from the Lord, revision is unnecessary.

So important is the subject of spiritual manifestation and so great the interest is becoming—not only throughtout the Pentecostal Movement, but in most denominations—that the matter needs to be studied carefully and deeply and the mind of the Lord clearly sought so that the scriptural manifestation might be clearly understood and operated.

The Church needs the Pentecostal power but it also requires the wisdom of the Word in order to use the sacred manifestations of the Spirit to the glory of God, avoiding all that is not edifying to the Church.

We present this volume to the public in the hope that it will prove interesting and profitable, praying the Lord to confirm to the hearts of the readers all that is in perfect accord with the eternal Word.

In writing this book I have been especially indebted to my brother John Carter for his critical comments—always valuable and never refused—which have greatly assisted in its compilation.

Also, I am deeply indebted to Mrs. Gibson, of London, for her excellent work in typing and re-typing the whole manuscript.

H. C.

—1—

The Gifts of the Spirit

Our reading is 1 Corinthians 12:1-11: "I would not have you ignorant concerning spiritual gifts." What an appalling ignorance there is today regarding the gifts of the Spirit! How seldom, if ever, in some churches is this chapter referred to; yet the apostle Paul said he would not have us ignorant concerning them. The gifts of the Holy Spirit are a legacy to the church: they are gifts which our blessed Lord bequeathed when He died upon the cross of Calvary. He poured out the Holy Spirit from heaven when He ascended, and enriched His church with gifts of the Spirit of God. A legacy indeed—and who is not interested in legacies!

I remember how, before I went to India, I was included in a will. I was told to come and hear the will read. I said to myself, "This is God's way of providing the money that I shall need to go to India; my fare will now be paid." So I went and heard the will read, and I received my legacy, and when I picked up the five pounds that had been left to me (barely enough to buy a pair of shoes!) I knew that was not the only way God was going to provide. But in any case, we become interested if it's a legacy; if someone has actually remembered us in his will.

The Lord Jesus Christ left us a legacy, and we ought to be extremely interested in it. He has left us gifts of the Holy Ghost, and concerning these spiritual gifts we ought not to be ignorant, because ignorance will rob us of what we could otherwise possess and use.

I remember years ago hearing that celebrated preacher F. B. Meyer tell a story about Charles Haddon Spurgeon which I shall never forget. He said that Mr. Spurgeon was a bighearted man. Because he loved to interest himself in poor people, he had almshouses connected with his tabernacle, and he would make pastoral visits in these apartments where the old people lived. One old lady had brought all her belongings that were so sentimentally valuable to her (but not to anybody else), such as an old faded photograph, a couple of china dogs on the mantelpiece, and the clock that wouldn't go. Mr. Spurgeon would go around the room inspecting the treasures.

In this old lady's apartment he saw on the wall a piece of paper with some writing. Mr. Spurgeon asked the old lady, "What is this that you have framed?" She said, "Sir, that reminds me of an old man that I nursed years ago. He was a patient old man, and when he was dying he said, 'What can I give you to show my appreciation of all that you've done for me?' And, Sir, he wrote his name on that piece of paper and that's why I put it in the frame; it reminds me of the old man." Mr. Spurgeon said, "Could I borrow this? I will take very great care of it." She said, "Oh, but that's very dear to me; I would not like to lose that slip of paper with the old man's name on." But finally he persuaded her to let him have it. He removed it from the frame and took it to the bank. Maybe you have already guessed that this dear old lady had framed a check!

Charles Spurgeon said to the bank manager, "Do you know anything about this money?" and the bank manager said, "It has been lying here for a long time and nobody has ever claimed it." Spurgeon said, "I have come to claim it for an old lady who lives in the almshouses connected with the tabernacle."

He went back to the old lady and asked, "Why are you living in poverty here?" She said, "I have no money, Sir." He said, "Lady, you are mistaken; you are ignorant of what you possess; you have been worth money—hundreds of pounds—for a long time. That piece of paper is a check assigning you a lot of money." So he set her up in a comfortable little home of her own with her own money.

Is it not the same with spiritual things? If we are ignorant we lose the benefits God intended us to receive from the gifts that have been left us: "I would not have you ignorant concerning spiritual gifts." There is another side to ignorance concerning spiritual gifts; ignorance can be dangerous, decidedly so.

Brother Mark Draper, who was the District Superintendent for Northern California, told me a story about his boyhood. He said, "Brother Carter, when I was a boy and an automobile came along our street, it was an unusual sight." The boys would run after it just to look at the great moving machine. One day Mark Draper saw an automobile standing outside a house with the motor running, because in those days if you turned the motor off you were not quite sure it would start again. That car with the motor running presented a great temptation for the boy.

He said to himself, "I would love to get into that

car and make it go around the block." He got in but he did not know how to start it; he pulled this knob and pushed that and twisted the other, until it began to go. He got excited! The thing was really moving; all this mechanism was in motion, and internally he was in commotion. He was moving along now, holding the steering wheel, but extremely nervous, because he didn't know how he had started it, and didn't know how to stop it! He tried his best but could not get the thing to stop. He was in a panic now and decided as a drastic measure, that the sure way to make a car stop was to run it into a ditch! That is what he did; he ran it into a ditch, and it stopped. He got out and ran for his life, and didn't stop until he was out of sight.

Well, this is another case of ignorance, and also of the danger associated with it; you see, he was ignorant, and rather naughty too. But if he had been enlightened concerning automobiles he would not of necessity have done any damage; he only intended to take it around the block and put it back exactly where he had found it; but ignorance caused him to land that gentleman's car in the ditch. I want to say that ignorance concerning spiritual gifts has caused people to do drastic things, supposing they were being moved by the Spirit of God.

"Brethren, I would not have you ignorant. Ye know that ye were Gentiles, carried away unto these dumb idols, even as ye were led."

I've never been to Corinth; I flew over it in a plane on the way to Athens. My friend on the other side of the plane beckoned to me, and I went across and looked through his window; and there below was this very city of Corinth. I saw it from above; the apostle Paul preached in it on ground level. We came down at Athens where I had the privilege of preaching.

The apostle Paul is writing to these Corinthians, "Ye know that ye were Gentiles carried away unto these dumb idols," and I want you to note the term he uses of utter contempt—"these dumb idols"— for the idolater worships dumb idols. Yes, it has lips, but they never open; the idol has eyes, but they cannot see; the idol has ears, but it never hears anything or says anything—dumb idols! The apostle Paul is using this scornful term concerning the finest specimens, I presume, of sculpture that the world has ever seen; for some of the finest carvings were done by the Greek sculptors. They carved so perfectly that the statue of Venus (one of their goddesses) today is acknowledged as a leading work of art; and yet all this was prostituted to the one end of idolatry so that the people should have an object of worship.

The prophet Isaiah pours contempt upon the idolater. He says the idolater takes a piece of wood and carves it into an idol. From the same tree that he took the wood he takes kindling for the fire, and he burns some and says, "Aha, I am warm," and to the rest of the wood he bows down in worship. The idolater worships the work of his own hands; he makes his god, but the Christian worships the God who made him. There's the difference!

"Ye know that ye were Gentiles carried away." Now we come to a potent force, a power having nothing to do with the idol itself, but associated with it; for behind the idolatry of the world there is that awful power that rises from hell itself, leading people away from the worship of Jehovah to the worship of the works of their own hands—carried away, led, spiritistic movings, power—something awful demonic. "Ye know that ye were Gentiles carried away unto dumb idols, even as ye were led." Wherefore, he said, because they had known these psychic forces and powers, and because they had had these strange, uncanny, unholy leadings, he wanted them to understand clearly this fact: no man speaking under the power of the Holy Ghost will ever call Jesus accursed, because the Holy Spirit has come to magnify the Lord Jesus Christ, to glorify Him. No man speaking by the Spirit of God will ever call Jesus accursed when he is speaking under divine unction. When the Spirit of God comes mightily upon him, the utterance he gives, either in prophecy or in interpretation, will be divine and magnify our great Redeemer. Contrariwise, no man can say that Jesus is the Lord, but by the Holy Ghost.

Why? Because the devil wouldn't let him. The devil wouldn't let any of the evil spirits that worship him ever acclaim the lordship of the Redeemer. During World War II no one in English-speaking countries was permitted to speak well of Hitler and his forces for they were the enemy. The power that comes from hell will never magnify the Lord Jesus. But the Holy Spirit will. These Corinithians had been idolaters and had known the power that was not of God; there were, therefore, strange manifestations in their meetings at times, and so the apostle Paul lays down clearly that no man speaking by the Spirit of God will ever call Jesus accursed.

Now, he says there are diversities of gifts, but the same Spirit. There are nine gifts altogether: the word of wisdom, the word of knowledge, faith, gifts of healing, miracles, prophecy, discerning of spirits, divers

The Gifts of the Spirit

kinds of tongues, and the interpretation of tongues. These nine gifts of the Holy Spirit are diverse; for instance, what could be more diverse than the discerning of spirits and the working of miracles? And what a contrast there is between speaking with other tongues and gifts of healing; also, how diverse is the word of wisdom from the interpretation of tongues! There are gifts of mighty energy, gifts of power, and there are gifts that are telescopic which reveal the other world; there are gifts that are prophetic, inspirational, and gifts that are revelational.

Now, says the writer, it is the same Spirit who causes all of these to function. God has been pleased to put in nature a very simple illustration of this unity in diversity. Take, for instance, common water. I have a glass of it; it is a common commodity, but a very remarkable one. Do you know you can have water in the lump? You say "Brother Carter, we don't talk about water in the lump; we talk about ice." What is ice but a lump of solid water?

You can have this commodity floating about in the sky. What are clouds but water?

Then you can have water that comes down in pellets as if heaven were pea-shooting us. You say, "Brother Carter, we don't call those particles pellets, we call them hail." What is hail but frozen drops of water?

Then you can have all the trees covered with snow, all so white and beautiful they look like fairyland! I traveled across Siberia in wintertime, and some asked me, "What did it look like, Brother Carter?" I said, "Like snow!" I saw a roof occasionally sticking out of a great snowdrift, and felt sorry for those below. But snow is water.

Then there is an exquisite artist who will draw pictures on your windowpanes. You say, "Who is he?" Why, his name is Jack Frost, and he draws delightful pictures. Who is Jack Frost? Simply water in another manifestation. So, you can have water as rain, water as hail, water as snow, water as ice, water as steam, water as frost, and water as clouds; yet all these will, in a given temperature, flow as water.

How diverse they are, and yet they are all water. So we have an illustration of the verse, "There are diversities of gifts, but the same Spirit, and there are differences of administration, but the same Lord."

There is no uniformity with the Almighty as there is with man. When we erect a brick building, every brick is made in the same mold; pick up one and you've seen all of them. God never makes even two leaves the same, nor does He make two persons alike; no, not even if they are identical twins, such as we once had in our church in London.

There were a couple of young men who sat next to each other, and looked as much alike as two peas in a pod. I would look from one to the other, and the other to the one. I would ask myself, "Now which is which?" I said to the mother, "Can you tell them apart?" "Oh, yes," she said, "there are slight differences." It was difficult for me to say which was which. The schoolteacher had the same trouble. When one of them misbehaved, and the teacher said, "You have to stay in and write 500 lines," he would say to the other, "Write these lines for me, and I will write them for you next time," and the teacher did not know who was writing the lines.

I remember calling upon one of them. I knocked, and he came to the door. I said, "I want to see your

The Gifts of the Spirit

brother who hasn't been to church lately." He said, "I am afraid it is I you want to see." I couldn't tell those twins apart, but there were slight differences that the mother could tell. And so, God never makes two things alike.

With the ministry there are apostles, prophets, evangelists, pastors, and teachers, and how different they are! Why, an evangelist I knew could not suffer to sit down and listen to a Bible reading; he would want to be up and doing and say, "Brother Carter, when are you going to give the altar call?" We don't give altar calls in Bible studies unless we know there are sinners present.

The gifts differ; the ministries are different, and we shall see yet further variations. Look at the next verse: "There are diversities of operations"—the gifts are different in their function. To illustrate, let us take one of the gifts, the gift of working of miracles for instance. Moses had it when he went into Egypt, and God said, "Take thy rod," and he took his rod into Egypt; and God said, "Pass thy rod over the land," and the plagues began. When the sea was to be divided God said, "Pass thy rod over the sea," and the sea opened. When they needed water in the wilderness God said, "Smite the rock." He struck the rock, and water gushed out. It was the rod that God used in Moses' case; the working of miracles was associated with the rod.

Elijah had no rod; he had a mantle. When the mantle was upon him he was mighty; he could pray and fire would flash from heaven, and he could pray again with the mantle upon him and the rain would come. At the close of his ministry, when he came to the Jordan and wished to pass over, he wrapped the mantle together and smote the waters hither and thither; and with every smiting he put his foot down, step by step; he smote the waters out of the way, and they kept out until he and his servant Elisha had passed over Jordan. When they were on the other side, Elijah said to Elisha, "Ask what I will give thee," and Elisha said, "A double portion of thy spirit." He said, "If you see me when I am taken, it shall be yours." Elisha watched his master as the whirlwind blew and the chariots of fire and the horses of fire came galloping from the heavens, and watched his master when he was taken up in the whirlwind. Then he saw something coming down—what was it? It was the mantle, and when he put it on, he continued the ministry of his master. The last miracle that Elijah performed was, therefore, the first miracle that Elisha did; he took the mantle and bound it together and said, "Where is the God of Elijah?" and he smote the waters, and discovered that the power had been transferred to him. Elisha's power was associated with the mantle.

Let us take another man, Samson, who didn't have a mantle, neither did he have a rod; but he found the power of God coming into his very physique. It came through his body, through his muscles, and when he laid hold of things—my! It was a laying hold! He laid hold of the gates of Gaza and carried them on his back. He picked up the jawbone of an ass and slew a thousand men. At the end of his ministry, that sad end, he slew more through the power of the Spirit at his death than he did all through his lifetime. He laid hold of the two pillars of the temple of the god Dagon, and they broke under the mighty power that he exerted. Down crashed the whole temple killing so many. There is the difference: one man finds the working of miracles functioning through his being, another through a mantle, another through a rod, and so we can have the gifts functioning in different ways, and yet the same gift, for with the Almighty there is infinite variety.

Now the manifestation of the Spirit is given to every man to profit withal, which means that the manifestation is given for the general good of everybody. The Spirit of God is not given for personal enrichment. Let those men who are marvelously used of God with a healing ministry remember that God never gave His power to make a man rich and prominent; He gave it that the man might be a blessing to countless numbers, for the general good, the general blessing of the community and of the church. So, we need to be sanctified if we have the gifts and power of God. "Be ye holy that bear the vessels of the Lord."

—2—

The Word of Wisdom

"Now concerning spiritual gifts, brethren, I would not have you ignorant." "For to one is given by the Spirit the word of wisdom; to another the word of knowledge by the same Spirit" (1 Corinthians 12:1, 8).

The word of wisdom has nothing to do with our wisdom, any more than the speaking with tongues has any affinity with a linguistic gift, or the gifts of healing any relationship with the medical profession. We must draw the line of demarcation as clearly as possible between what is natural and what is supernatural, for there are natural gifts and there are supernatural gifts. There is a wisdom that is natural (for example, Ahithophel had it), and there is a wisdom that is divine which comes down from heaven. This is a manifestation of the Holy Spirit and it is the first and greatest gift of the nine—the word of God's wisdom imparted to us by the Spirit of God.

To show that it has nothing to do with our wisdom, let me give you a simple illustration. In London I have a lawyer to whom I go when I have legal difficulties. You know, when you buy buildings there are documents composed by lawyers, written so that no one can understand them, it would seem, unless he be

The Word of Wisdom

a lawyer himself! Having read the documents two or three times and not being sure I have the drift of their contents, I decide to get a word of wisdom from my lawyer; so I phone him.

The conversation goes something like this: "I have a deed relating to a property I am thinking of buying, but I don't know whether to go ahead with the purchase. Would you please give me some advice?"

"Will you read it to me?"

I read the whole document. Then I wait. What for? For the word of wisdom from my lawyer.

Now mark, it is not a gift of wisdom. There is no gift of wisdom promised in the Bible; God only offers us the gift of "a word of wisdom."

The lawyer gives me a word of wisdom. He does not give me a gift of wisdom; his brains do not come through the wires into my ear and into my skull! No! If he gave me a gift of wisdom I would never need to go to him again—I would use the gift— but he gives me the gift of a word. Well, he does not exactly give me a gift; I have to pay for it!

We are offered, in this first great manifestation of the Spirit of God, the *word* of wisdom. God gives us a directive word; it is the word of His wisdom; it is not the word of our wisdom at all. You may ask, "To whom has God ever given the word of His wisdom?" He has given it again and again; the Bible is full of instances.

You remember at the time of Noah, God spoke from heaven, "Noah, the end of all flesh is come before me... Make thee an ark" (Genesis 6:13, 14). And so God gave him the word of His wisdom, for God had decided what He would do with this world; He would destroy it; but He would preserve Noah, his wife, his sons, and their wives in an ark. So the word of God's wisdom revealed to Noah the way of his salvation. Whenever God speaks to a man directly, He is giving him a word of His wisdom.

He spoke to Jonah and said, "Go to Nineveh." Jonah didn't want to go, so he went in the opposite direction; he went to Joppa to take a boat across the Mediterranean to go to Spain. He had no wish to carry out the word of God's wisdom, to fulfill this commission from the Almighty to go and preach to the Ninevites. No! He would go and have a vacation in Spain, and stay there long enough for the Almighty to forget all about Nineveh, and then he would go back home! So he went to Joppa, got on the boat, paid his fare, and went to sleep; but there was a great storm. Jonah was an illogical man; he knew he was out of God's will; yet he expected the Almighty to blow gently with His wind and send the sailing vessel across the Mediterranean, carrying him positively out of the will of God.

God did blow! He blew a storm, and Jonah was in the storm. The sailors tried to row, but when God makes a storm, however hard you row, the storm follows you. They said, "Now, who is responsible?" They cast lots and the lot fell upon Jonah, and he had to own up that he was out of the will of God:

"The God of heaven has done this because of me."

"What shall we do?"

"Get rid of me; cast me into the sea."

But these sailors were friendly and sympathetic, so they went on rowing. However, they couldn't row out of God's will. They finally had to cast Jonah overboard, and he was not seen by them again. He slid down a very dark passage and he came into a cabin with no portholes and a very poor ventilating system. If anybody ever suffered from claustrophobia Jonah must surely have been the one; he was three days and three nights (but they were all nights) in the fish's belly.

The Lord directed the fish back to land. That was very convenient for Jonah, for when the fish, unable to digest the morsel he had swallowed, vomited him up, it was on dry land!

Then came the word of God again to Jonah, "Go to Nineveh," and this time he went. He had had enough of Joppa, and ships, and fishes, and darkness; he went and fulfilled the word of God's wisdom, and there was a great revival.

That's the way God speaks to men. The word of wisdom has always been directive. He said to the man of God during Jeroboam's reign, "Go to Bethel and cry against the altar," and the man of God went, and cried against the altar according to the word of the Lord.

Sometimes people think that they have the word of God's wisdom, and they are mistaken. They have, perhaps, a good imagination; they have peculiar leadings; they become superspiritual or mystical to a degree that isn't healthy.

I knew a good man—he was a good man, but he went wrong regarding his leadings. He thought God was speaking to him all the time; he imagined God spoke to him every ten minutes or so of the day, telling him what to do. This man declared that God said to him, "Arise, my servant, go to such a mission across the city." He arose, dressed himself and went. He couldn't go on the streetcar because he hadn't any money. It was a number of miles to the mission—perhaps ten or twelve miles to walk—but he went. When he got there, the mission was closed. There he stood outside, and he said, "Thy servant has obeyed Thee, Lord. Thou didst say, 'Arise and go to the Mission,' and lo, I have come and it is closed. Now what is the word of the Lord to His servant?" And the Lord said, "Arise and return home."

Isn't that absolutely ridiculous? We make a laughingstock of the things of God when we act like that; we think we are receiving leadings only to find they are not from the Lord.

I'll tell you of a leading. It was the year 1919. Six of us were gathered together for an hour of prayer in a pastor's home in the north of London. The Lord spoke to us, "Gather My people together, saith the Lord; gather from the north, and from the south, from the east and from the west, and build for Me. It shall come upon horses, and mules, camels and dromedaries, chariots and wheels a great company, and ye shall build for Me, and there shall be heaps of money, heaps upon heaps." I heard someone laughing, and it was the pastor in whose home we were praying (he was still on his knees). He was holding his sides and rocking with laughter. I said, "What are you laughing for?" He said, "The money, heaps upon heaps; I saw it coming like sand to a point," and he laughed again, and we all had a good laugh.

I suppose living by faith has gone out of fashion in these days, but living by faith, as we understood it then, was having no fixed income; the pastor had a ministry box at the door in his church, and I had a box at the door in my church. So, to hear the Lord talking about heaps of money was something thrilling.

My friend laughed until his sides hurt, and then we all went on praying.

When we gathered for the midday meal, the pastor's wife had to be told about the message of the Lord. The pastor said to her, "My dear, what do you think the Lord said to us this morning? He said we would have heaps of money." I can see her now as she clapped her hands together, saying, "Praise the Lord, may it come quickly!" We all had another good laugh, and we finished our meal.

That evening the pastor and I had an invitation to supper at a friend's house in the country. About nine o'clock I said to the pastor, "We shall need to tell our host we must be going." I have never been one to keep late hours.

Our host said, "Wait a minute, don't go yet; I have something to tell you." I settled back in my chair, hoping the matter would not take too long to discuss. He said, "You know, I am a businessman, and I have not paid my tithes to the Lord for a long time. God spoke to me and said, 'Lay the money at the apostles' feet.'" So I said, "You have to find the apostles before you can discover their feet!"

He did not take any notice of my remark but went on, "I am going to give it to you two brethren."

My friend said, "How much do you think it will be?"

"I am not quite sure; it will be something more than 2,000 pounds."[1]

I gave the pastor a nudge and said, "You remember what God said to us this morning?" "Yes," he exclaimed aloud, "the Lord said we should have heaps upon heaps of money."

---
[1] Formerly, about $9,600.

Our host said, "Well, here's the first heap," and he gave us 2,400 pounds.[2] A pound was worth more then than it is today—a lot more!

"Ah," you say, "that was wonderful!" Yes, it was wonderful, but mark the message had three parts to it. The first part said, "Gather My people together, from the north, and from the south, from the east and from the west." Then part two, "It shall come upon horses and mules, and camels and dromedaries, and chariots and wheels." Then the third part, "There shall be heaps and heaps of money." Within twelve hours the third part of the message was partly fulfilled; we got the first heap.

You say, "What about the other two parts?" Well, we could not see how the first part would be fulfilled and we waited. Then it came; in 1921 a call came for me to take charge of the Pentecostal Bible School in London, and the students came from the north, and from the south, from the east, and from the west.

You say, "What about the middle part, horses and mules, and camels?" From that Bible school in Hampstead, where I was principal for over twenty-seven years, there are students ministering in over twenty different countries of the world where there are camels, dromedaries, horses, chariots, and wheels. In over twenty different countries of the world the students are working. The word of wisdom is always specifically and marvellously fulfilled when it is from God. His plan for us in 1919 was to gather together and send out young men, and we should have heaps of money to do it with.

Moses is standing in the desert minding sheep. He

---

[2] Formerly, about $11,500

The Word of Wisdom

had been in the palace in Egypt, brought up among the aristocracy, and now he is a shepherd. The shepherd sees a bush burning with fire; he hears the voice of the Almighty speaking out of the flame; and he receives a commission from God. We read about Moses' call in the third chapter of Exodus.

The voice of God says, "I am come down to deliver my people, now therefore go into Egypt." It was God's word; God's directive word; God's word of wisdom telling Moses what to do. Moses went and the children of Israel were delivered.

When Moses came to Mount Sinai and God called him up into the mount, he was to see the finger of God moving upon the stone, leaving an incision on the hard stone, and there before his eyes the Ten Commandments were written in tables of stone. He was receiving the word of God's administrative wisdom.

All Messianic prediction in the Old Testament (indeed, all prediction) is a part of the word of wisdom, for what God purposed to do concerning the Messiah was to make known His plan for the world, and so in His wisdom He revealed His purpose. He showed where the Messiah would be born, how He would grow up as a root out of dry ground, how He would suffer, and eventually be rejected and die for the sins of the people.

You say, "Does not prediction constitute prophecy?" The simple gift of prophecy contains no revelation; it is to "edification, exhortation and comfort." You ask, "Does not the Bible talk sometimes about a man prophesying when he is giving a prediction?" It does, because the term prophecy can be used both specifically and in a general way.

We may use terms both specifically and generally.

For instance, if I said to you, "Come and have some tea," you would take that in a general sense; you would think, "He means, come and have a cup of that stimulating beverage with a little bread and butter and a slice of cake—or other food suitable for the occasion."

But if you said to a grocer, "I want some tea," he would think of dried leaves in a package. Speaking specifically, "tea" is one thing; speaking generally it can be a beverage plus a whole meal.

Now, prophecy can be used specifically, that is, as a simple gift to edification, exhortation or comfort, or it can be used as a general term for the manifestation of any of the spoken gifts; so that if a man is said to prophesy, he may be giving a word of wisdom—but that is using the word "prophecy" in a general sense.

Oh, there is so much we could say about this word of wisdom. Remember, the Lord Jesus Christ told Peter what he was going to do, how he would deny Him. He lamented over the destruction of Jerusalem which He saw coming. God sees the future, and when He reveals to an individual what He sees and what He has determined, He gives to that person the word of wisdom.

The word of wisdom is the greatest of all the gifts of the Holy Spirit. See how it can span the ages. Enoch, the seventh from Adam, prophesied (here is the word in the general sense): "The Lord cometh with ten thousand of his saints to execute judgment upon . . . all that are ungodly," and so on (Jude 14, 15). The prediction has not been fulfilled yet, but we are certain the Lord is coming and the word will be fulfilled.

You say, "How old does a person have to be before he can have a revelation from God?" How old does a person need to be before he can speak with other tongues? Oh, you say, "He speaks with other tongues by the Spirit." Well, he receives revelation by the Spirit also, and to illustrate this point, let me tell you of a little boy whose mother dedicated him to the work of God.

Samuel lived in the Temple with Eli, the priest. He was in bed one night and heard a voice saying, "Samuel," and being a prompt, obedient little boy he jumped out of bed and ran down the corridor and said to Eli, "Here am I." Eli answered, "I didn't call you, go and lie down."

That incident was repeated, and again Eli told the boy to return to his bed.

But the voice came the third time, "Samuel," and the boy jumped out of bed and ran to Eli again. Eli thought, "Oh, he is hearing the voice of God," and he said, "If you hear the voice again, say, 'Speak, Lord, for thy servant heareth.'" So, the voice came again, "Samuel," and he said, "Speak; for thy servant heareth."

Then God spoke to the boy and gave him a revelation of the judgment that was coming upon Eli's house because he had not brought up his sons as he should, and because they were profane. The next morning Eli said to Samuel, "Tell me what the Lord said to you." He was afraid, but he told him, and Eli said, "It is the Lord."

The word of God's wisdom can come to a child, because it is God's wisdom and not the child's wisdom.

The word of wisdom is the greatest of all the manifestations of the Spirit of God, because it is directive—

it tells you what God would have you do, and there is nothing more important than to be directed by heaven.

Oh, may God direct us!

—3—

The Word of Knowledge

Our reading is from the book of the prophet Isaiah 32:13-19.

Then 1 Corinthians 12:8: "For to one is given by the Spirit the word of wisdom; to another the word of knowledge by the same Spirit."

What wonderful variety there is in the gifts of the Spirit! That variety can be seen as we compare the gifts of extraordinary power and demonstration with the gifts of remarkable light and revelation. This gift of revelation we are now considering is the communication by God of the word of knowledge. The word of knowledge has nothing to do with human knowledge; if it had, it wouldn't be a manifestation of the Spirit; it would be a manifestation of our intellect. We want a manifestation of the Spirit of God, and the word of knowledge is the communication by the Holy Spirit of the knowledge of the Lord.

So often this blessed gift has been associated with the natural knowledge acquired by study of the Word. As one dear lady said to me, "Brother Carter, you must have the word of knowledge, you know the Bible so well." It makes one smile a little. It is not a knowledge of the Word that comes from study, but the word of knowledge comes by the Spirit of God in revelation.

I repeat, the word of knowledge is the communication by the Spirit of God of that knowledge that is an attribute of Deity; it is so vast, shoreless, and fathomless that we call it Omniscience—God's all-knowledge. He knows every star in the heavens, and they are innumerable. I have read books on astronomy, and my head reels when I think of those astronomical numbers—millions and trillions of stars, great floating universes with billions of stars in each galaxy—and yet the Bible says God calls them all by names. He has named every star in the heavens; but let us come down to earth—we will get lost up there—let's set our feet on terra firma. What does God know of human affairs? God knows every nation, for the Bible says He works in the midst of the nations to set up and to put down; but God not only knows every nation, He knows every person in every nation. Here is a verse to prove it: "The man Moses was very meek, above all the men which were upon the face of the earth" (Numbers 12:3). Now, that is a superlative statement! "Moses was very meek, above all that were upon the face of the earth," so the hearts of all men living at that time must have been examined individually by the Almighty before God could proclaim that the meekest man of that day was Moses. So God knows every man, and God knows more than that—He knows the footsteps of every person. The Psalmist says, "Thou knowest my downsitting and my uprising...and art acquainted with all my ways" (Psalm 139:2, 3). God knows every step we take—He saw you come into this building tonight, saw the seat you sat on, and He will watch when you get

The Word of Knowledge

up and go out. God knows every footstep; and if you would like to go further than that, God knows every hair on our heads.

Now, if God is pleased, for the fulfillment of His purpose, to communicate to us, by the Spirit, something of this amazing knowledge, and to let us partake, even though to an infinitesimal extent, of this amazing omniscience, then He gives to us a word of His knowledge.

Why should God give to us a fragment of His knowledge? I will give an instance from Scripture. You remember that the children of Israel had backslidden; they wanted a king so that they might be like the nations. God didn't want them to be like the nations; He wanted them to be an example to the nations; but He granted them a king, and Saul was the one chosen. Saul at that time was a humble man, and when the day of his coronation came he was so shy that when all the people gathered together to witness the coronation he went and hid himself. Nobody could find him! That produced a very embarrassing situation for Samuel, for the people would say, "Samuel, where is the king?" Samuel would say, "I don't know. We have looked everywhere and we cannot find him." "Samuel, what are you going to do? We have come from our cities and towns, and from our farms and hamlets; we have come from great distances to see this man crowned, and you say you cannot find him? You must find him!"

Well, what can a man do in such a predicament? He can pray, and that is what Samuel did—he prayed, perhaps something like this: "O God, Thou who knowest where every person is in the whole world, wilt Thou be pleased to show me where Saul is?"

God was pleased to answer him, saying, "Saul has hid himself in the stuff." I don't know what the stuff was, but they knew, because they went to the stuff and they got him out.

Now you see how the word of knowledge saved the situation; Saul was lost and nobody could find him, but God communicated that infinitesimal portion of His omniscience which was sufficient to locate Saul. It doesn't matter how small may be the knowledge communicated, it is miraculous if it is a word of knowledge by divine revelation. For instance, when you go to the seashore with your children and they take their sand buckets and spades, and your little boy puts his bucket into the sea and brings it back full of water, he has got a little of the ocean in his bucket—very little of course. We might say what he has is infinitesimal in quantity, but in quality it is precisely the same as the rest of it; for all you have to do to fill an ocean is to take the little bucket, fill it, and pour it out enough times. There is nothing different in the quality of it, but only in the quantity. So, if God communicates to you one little drop of His amazing knowledge, you have a positive word of knowledge. In quality it is precisely the same as omniscience in quantity, infinitesimal.

Ahijah, the blind prophet, was living during the reign of the wicked king Jeroboam. Jeroboam's son fell ill and he said to his wife, the queen, "Disguise thyself... there is the prophet... he shall tell thee what shall become of the child." (1 Kings 14:2, 3).

Now, she didn't need to disguise herself for the prophet's sake, because he was blind; but others might have run before and said, "The queen is coming to see you." As she was going down to the prophet, the

Lord spoke to Ahijah. He said, "Ahijah, the wife of Jeroboam is coming down to see you about her son." It was the word of God's knowledge which He communicated to the man who could not see. When Ahijah heard her footsteps at the door he said, "Come in, thou wife of Jeroboam." It must have been disconcerting, after she had gone to the trouble of disguising herself, to hear the prophet boldly calling out her name.

Now this word of knowledge is very wonderful, but we must not assume to have what we do not positively possess; for instance, some people have a critical faculty, and they will attribute their faultfinding to a gift of the Spirit. A man I knew in Montreal was a very fine person. He had what I suppose every woman wants: a head of wavy hair. One day a lady came with a very solemn face. He said, "Sit down, Sister." She said, "No, I won't sit down in this place."

"What is it, Sister?" he asked.

"God has sent me to rebuke you," she said. "I have to rebuke you for having a permanent wave put in your hair."

He said, "Do you think I have had it permanently waved?"

"I know it; God has shown me!" she exclaimed.

He said, "Come with me, Sister," and he took her into the kitchen, and put his head under the tap. He soaked his hair good and wet, and then rubbed it with a towel. He got a comb, and back the hair went into its waves; she could see that it was natural.

She said, "I am sorry; I have made a mistake."

Don't be quick to criticize, and be particularly careful in claiming a word of knowledge. You may shame man and shame the Almighty at the same time by your folly; but since I have told you an unfortunate incident, I must give you a true manifestation of this word of knowledge.

I want to take you back to when the Primitive Methodist revival was sweeping over England; when churches were being opened at the rate of one a day; when men and women mighty in prayer were pleading with heaven for souls, and seeing them converted. There was a man among them named John Oxterby, well known for his prayer life, and to whom people went in their trouble.

There was one poor woman whose son was out at sea on a sailing boat, and there had been, of late, some severe storms at sea. The boat was long overdue, and what did the mother think? She was like all mothers; they worry about their sons and their daughters until they know they are safe.

In those days there was no radar, no radio between ship and ship, and the mother was worried; so she went to John Oxterby.

"Mr. Oxterby, will you pray about my son? He is out at sea and he should have been here days and days ago, and there have been some awful storms at sea. Will you pray and ask God if he is safe or not?"

"I will, Ma'am, I will do that," and so he prayed. I presume that he prayed at night, and now something was happening: the dark shadows were being chased away by a lovely light, a light that showed him the broad expanse of the open sea—great blue waters covered with white caps—and a boat, a sailing vessel, coming along in full sail.

"Is this the boat, Lord?" "It is." "Thank You."

"Is the boy there? Ah, there he is." He can see

The Word of Knowledge

the boy; he can see the ship; he can see the sails swelling in the wind; he can see the wash the ship leaves behind it, and he can see the mighty bow cutting through the waters.

"Mr. Oxterby, did you pray about my boy?"

"I did, Ma'am, and he is all right. He is coming home, and he will be here soon."

The mother replied, "Thank you, Mr. Oxterby; I hope that is right."

The ship came in and the boy was safe.

In those days the people could doubt almost as well as they can today. They got their heads together and said, "I wonder if he made it up; I wonder if he imagined it; I wonder if he sees visions like that. Well, we can soon find out. We will put him on the spot."

So they took him down to the harbor and asked him to point out the ship.

"Mr. Oxterby, did you say you saw the ship with that boy on board in a vision?"

"I did."

"Was it a clear vision, or a little misty? You saw the ship clearly? You never saw the ship before, but you saw it clearly in the vision?"

"I did."

"Would you mind coming down to the harbor with us?"

"Why?"

"There are sixteen ships there, and it is one of them; you might point it out to us."

John Oxterby had never seen the ship, except in vision. He looked over the harbor and pointed, "That's the one." He pointed to the right one.

This gift of the word of knowledge is a communication from heaven by the Spirit of God of things that are on earth. It can be so clear that you know every detail. But it is a gift that is not appreciated by some because it can expose sin.

When Naaman, the great Syrian general, came seeking and receiving healing of Elisha, he was amazed at the miracle that had taken place in his body. He drove up to the prophet's home in his chariot with gold, silver, and garments to enrich the prophet out of gratitude for the miracle wrought. The man of God said, "Nothing, thank you."

"Nothing?"

"Nothing," and he sent him away, for Elisha wanted him to know that he was saved by grace through faith. So he departed to his own country saying, "The God of Israel is a liberal God."

But the prophet's servant, Gehazi, was standing by, and he had a spirit of covetousness. He thought, "What a mistake; fancy my master sending this man home with all that money; think of the money we could use and the money we have prayed for! I will run after him," and he did. It is amazing how quickly people can run when they are after money. He caught up with the chariot, and he said, "Sir, my master has sent me to say that he has some visitors and needs some money." The grateful Naaman sent two of his servants with a talent of silver, and Gehazi told them where to put it; so he hid it and went and stood in his master's presence.

"Gehazi, where have you been?"

"Been, sir? I haven't been anywhere."

"You haven't been anywhere?"

"No, sir."

"Did not my heart go with you when you ran after

The Word of Knowledge

the chariot, Gehazi? Is this the time to get olive yards and vineyards, and men and women servants? Is this the time to enrich yourself? The leprosy of Naaman shall cleave to you." In a moment he was a leper as white as snow.

Let me remind you also of an incident in the ministry of Jesus. The woman at the well was greatly surprised when He began to talk about the life she was living. Then came the revelation about herself: "Thou hast had five husbands, and he whom thou now hast is not thy husband." Yes, the word of knowledge can expose sin.

But let me tell you what I consider to be the greatest instance of the word of knowledge in the Bible. It is in the Book of Isaiah, and these are the words: "Is there a God beside me? yea there is no God beside me" (Isaiah 45:5). There is a communication of knowledge, of God's knowledge, and before that word could be communicated to the prophet Isaiah, the entire universe had to be searched!

That is the greatest word of knowledge that I know, and now shall I tell you the smallest word of knowledge that I know? It came from a friend of mine, a man who passed on some years ago. He was a workingman, a devout man who had a large family. He bought his boy a fountain pen, and the boy went to a cricket field and lost it. He came home and told his father.

He said, "Son, take me to the field." The father knelt in a corner of the field. He prayed, "O God, where is the fountain pen?"

Here was a man who believed God knew where the fountain pen was. The Lord answered, "The fountain pen is under the tree at the other side of the field."

So he said to his son, "Get up, your fountain pen is under that tree."

They found the fountain pen right under that tree. I call that the smallest word of knowledge I know. Between these two you can have an amazing variety of extraordinary instances that bring glory to God, inspiration to man, blessing to the church, and fear to the sinners in Zion; and cause God to be honored through the manifestation of His Spirit. Oh, let us pray for more of the Spirit of God in manifestation.

—4—

Faith

Let us take for our reading 1 Corinthians 14:6-14 and 1 Corinthians 12:9.

The gift of faith is a wonderful gift that has not been fully understood, we fear, because it is generally confused with ordinary faith, or saving faith. Here is a gift that is mighty; for, in its position in the category of spiritual manifestations it comes before the gifts of healing and the working of miracles.

"But," one may say, "what could be greater than a miracle, which must be a stupendous manifestation of the power of God?" Well, that is what I will endeavour to demonstrate.

The gift of faith can be defined as faith imparted by the Spirit of God for protection in times of danger, or for divine provision, or it may include the ability to impart blessing.

Remember how Elijah was fed by ravens. God said to him, "Turn thee eastward, and hide thyself by the brook Cherith ... I have commanded the ravens to feed thee" (1 Kings 17:3,4). There might easily have been a doubt in his mind as to whether the ravens would actually feed him; these carnivorous creatures generally spend all their time feeding themselves, apparently eating from morning to night. How could Elijah expect ravens to bring food to him, the hiding prophet? But God said, "I have commanded the ravens to feed thee." So Elijah was to hide, with no other means of support, no friends to help him, no opportunity to do a little shopping for himself; he was to depend upon the Almighty to send these birds to feed him. At first it must have been a great test of faith; Elijah would be saying his prayers in hiding, waiting for his breakfast to come; for God had said, "Bread and flesh in the morning and bread and flesh in the evening," and that he would drink from the brook.

You do not have to be a vegetarian to be mighty with God, evidently. Bread and flesh in the morning, and bread and flesh in the evening! I do not think we need two meals of meat if we live an indoor life, but out in the open one needs more meat.

Let us imagine the first morning as he was waiting for his breakfast to come on the wing. He would doubtless look into the heavens, watching for a bird flying near. He did not know whether the bread or the meat would arrive first. Perhaps the bread would come first, and he would begin to feel gratitude in his heart.

One might say, "Brother Carter, was it hygienic to eat bread and meat that had been pecked by birds?" You might refuse to eat a piece of cheese if a mouse had nibbled at it. Here was a man whose every piece of bread and meat had been pecked by a bird first. What about germs? God would have dealt with them; for if God sends the food, the provision will be wholesome.

What did Elijah do to be fed by the ravens? He

Faith

had to exercise the faith which God had given him. If he did not believe, the birds would not come, or the bread and meat would be devoured on the way. Gifts given must be exercised.

Faith is a gift that enables one to believe for God to undertake in a supernatural way.

Daniel was thrown into the lions' den because he would not cease praying to his God. There was the test. He must either stop praying or be cast into the lions' den. (Some people stop praying without any threat of a lions' den awaiting them.) Daniel opened his window toward the east and prayed to his God. As a result, he was committed to the den of lions. What did Daniel do in the den? He did nothing! At least nothing that was evident; but God had given him faith, faith so mighty that the lions could not touch him. There was protection from danger. You ask, "How does this gift differ from the working of miracles?" That is a good question, and we must endeavor to answer it.

You remember that Samson, when he was going down to make arrangements for his marriage to a Philistine young woman, was met by a lion. What did Samson do when the beast sprang at him? The Spirit of the Lord came mightily upon him, and he tore the lion as if it had been a goat; he flung its carcass by the wayside, and went on his journey. That was a miracle; that was the working of miracles in contradistinction to the experience of Daniel who did not touch a beast in the lions' den. If they had put Samson in the lions' den he might have cracked all their jaws as soon as possible, and then lain down to rest on one of the carcasses until they let him out in the morning.

Daniel and Elijah did nothing but trust. It was that mighty sustained faith that brought into operation the powers of the world to come.

With Daniel, God sent His angel and stopped the lions' mouths. That is the gift of faith—God doing the work *for* you. The working of miracles is God doing the work *through* you. So, if God sends His angel to do anything for you, then you have the gift of faith. Notice how much greater the gift of faith is than the working of miracles because the working of miracles is limited to what God can do through a human vessel, but the gift of faith is unlimited; it can call on omnipotent powers if you have faith and require their services. They will be at your disposal as you exercise the gift of faith.

Jesus said, "Thinkest thou that I cannot now pray to my Father, and he shall presently give me more than twelve legions of angels?" (Matthew 26:53). Faith can expect the help of heaven's legions when required.

The gift of faith is very wonderful, but let us think about faith from its various standpoints.

You know, there is a natural faith which has nothing to do with the Spirit of God at all. This is the faith that a person has when he goes into an airplane for the first time, and this is the faith that people do not have when they say, "I am not going in; I won't fly unless I can keep one foot on the ground!"

Let me tell you a little story about flying. In the early days of flying between London and Paris, they had big planes for those days—forty seaters, and that was a colossal number of passengers for planes which were made of wood and canvas. On one occasion, soon after one of the great four-engine biplanes rose up to make

Faith

its way to Paris, a propeller snapped (propellers were made of wood) and when that propeller broke it damaged another, and these two broke a third, so there was only one good propeller left functioning. The pilot decided to make a forced landing.

A woman in the plane went into hysterics; she screamed and ran up and down the aisle in panic. There was a man on that plane who was used to driving cars. Every time he went into a race he knew his life was in danger. He had stared death in the face so often, he had adopted the motto, "Be killed calmly." With a voice of authority he said to the woman, "Sit down and give the pilot a chance!" Such was the authority in his voice—something so commanding—the woman stopped rushing up and down and went to her seat. The pilot brought the plane down and nobody was hurt.

That was natural faith. The man did not make any mention of the name of God—it was all natural—but it was a faith that could face danger and be peaceful; it could hold him steady and inspire all in the plane so that they kept calm.

Now let us talk about the faith of devils, for devils believe. James said, "Hast thou faith? the devils believe and tremble." Why is it that devils, who believe in God, do not get converted? Because they have a faith that does not alter them; if you have a faith that does not change your life, there is something sadly wrong with your faith; you have a faith such as devils have—you may tremble, but you do not change. There are people who say, "Yes, I believe in Jesus Christ," but their lives contradict their statement; their lives have not been changed. Their faith is of no value at all. There is no atheism in hell; they believe in God down in hell and tremble.

But there is another kind of faith: saving faith. If we believe that Jesus Christ died upon the cross of Calvary, that faith cleanses us from sin. He was raised for our justification. We believe that He ascended to heaven to plead for us before the Father, and it brings gratitude to the heart. That faith changes a person, and that is saving faith: "Believe on the Lord Jesus Christ and thou shalt be saved" (Acts 16:31).

There is also the fruit of faith. Faith is a fruit of the Spirit: "love, joy, peace, longsuffering, gentleness, goodness, faith, meekness, temperance." The more fruit you bear unto God in the Spirit, the more you believe. It is the fruit of the Spirit to believe, and to keep on believing more and more.

There are people who have been saved, and they have only believed one thing; namely, that Jesus died upon the cross. There are a lot of other things they cannot believe. They cannot believe that Jonah was swallowed by the whale (they say that story is too much to "swallow"); but as they grow in grace, they come to accept things they could not believe at first, and go on believing more and more as the fruit of the Spirit develops in their lives.

Then there is the gift of faith. This remarkable gift brings into operation the powers of the world to come; it causes God to work *for* you and not merely *through* you. God sends His angels to work for you, and, while we are talking about angels working for one, let me refer you to Elijah and mention three points from his life—all regarding faith, and, in a sense, a progression of faith that developed great spiritual strength.

First, he was fed by the ravens; he did nothing but wait and believe for the birds to come. I presume that each morning and evening he could see his food being brought by God's messengers in the air.

Later, he left Cherith and went to Zarephath, where he prophesied that the widow's barrel of meal would not waste. Here a miracle of provision takes place; there is divine supply. What is Elijah doing to bring this about? Nothing! The barrel of meal is supplying his needs. Could he see the meal coming? No! he could not see the meal coming into the barrel; it would have a lid on for hygienic reasons, and so there was a further degree of faith required in believing for what he could not see.

Later, he ran into the desert because of Jezebel's threat to take his life, and lay under the juniper tree, where an angel came and made him a cake. Then he rested and again woke up, and the angel made him another cake. When he had the second cake he rose up and went in the strength of that food forty days and nights, not eating or drinking, across the burning desert. Here we have the greatest degree of faith.

First, divine provision was carried visibly by the birds; then it came by the barrel, every day's supply coming unseen, and finally, he receives a supply of food sufficient to last for forty days, and he walks across the desert in the strength of the meat he received from the angel's hands.

Oh, what a gift is this gift of faith! I suppose if it were more in operation in the church today stupendous things would take place, as they have when men have dared to believe God in the past.

I marvel when I think of Hudson Taylor and his

China Inland Mission work, how he evangelized such a great part of China and never asked people for money, and would not allow his workers to ask for it. He said, "Pray for it." When we pray for money, we don't ask men for it; we get it from heaven.

Some people have told me, "Brother Carter, if ever you are in need, let us know," but I have never let them know. What does the Bible say? "Cease from man whose breath is in his nostrils" (Isaiah 2:22). It means that the rich will die one day, and it is better to depend upon the Lord whose breath is not in His nostrils.

So faith is a wonderful thing. Peter had it when he was in prison, the night before his execution. How do I know? Because he went to sleep. By the decree of King Herod he was to be decapitated the next day. This had been arranged; it was decreed; but Peter went to sleep.

Without being morbid, let's think about it. Suppose you knew that tomorrow you were to die; how much sleep would you have tonight? You might take aspirin, but how much sleep would you have if you were to be hanged tomorrow? You would be hanged a thousand times in thought during the night! But here is a man who has gone to sleep. The angel came into the cell and even the flashing glory of the angel's presence did not wake him up. So the angel smote him on the hip; the chains fell off and God brought him out. There is faith!

How did he have that stupendous faith to be able to go to sleep the night before his decreed execution? Because Jesus had said to him, "When thou art old another shall gird thee." Peter would say to himself, "Herod says I am to die tomorrow, but I'm

Faith 45

not old yet, and Jesus told me when I am old another shall gird me. Good-night everybody!" So he went to sleep on the sure word of Christ.

Oh, what a gift it is!

Years ago I saw a church for sale in London and purposed to buy it, but I didn't have the necessary 2,000 pounds.[1] A few days before, the lawyer had written to say the deeds would be signed on the morrow and would I kindly bring the money along.

God had given me 40 pounds[2], and then I had another sum of money (I forget how much) but now I needed the rest. I thought, "It will come through the mail" (that is like food coming on the wing), so I went to see what the morning post brought me. There was nothing. In the afternoon the same again. There was an evening delivery also but nothing came—nothing financial! The next day I must sign the deeds and I didn't have the money. What should I do? I decided to go to bed. Then, on my way, I noticed that on the doormat there lay an old yellow envelope. It was addressed to me. I looked inside; there was no letter, but it was full of Bank of England notes. I got quite excited. I sat down and began to count. There were 1,000 pounds[3] and a scrap of paper inside with the words: "For the church." The donor had been his own postman. God provided the money and we secured the church.

I think one of the modern-day instances of the gift of faith is the life of George Múller, who fed thousands of orphans and never appealed to anyone for money. He used to send out a quarterly report to those interested, and this usually brought contributions. On one occasion, however, his funds were

---
[1] Formerly, about $9,600. [2] Formerly, about $190. [3] Formerly, about $4,800.

exhausted and he decided not to send the report out.

Did God fail him? The members of his staff said, "Mr. Múller, we have no bread for the children; what shall we do?" "Put them around the table," Mr. Múller replied.

All the children marched in and sat down. The dear little children were sitting at the table and there was no bread. What could the man of God do now? Would God fail him? There was a knock at the door. A member of the staff came to Mr. Múller and said, "The local baker is at the door. He says he has made a mistake which he has never made before; he has baked two lots of bread and cannot dispose of both lots, so he wants to know if we can use a whole baking of bread for the children." Such faith! May God inspire us to trust more.

Let me tell you about "Holy Ann," a simple, trusting woman in Canada who knew God. She had trouble with one of her legs and the bone needed to be scraped. The doctor, for whom she was housekeeper, said she must have an egg a day. He didn't stop to think that it was the wrong time of the year to order eggs. Ann prayed, "Father, I need an egg a day," and lo, as she was sitting there in the kitchen, a hen appeared on the doorstep. The Lord said, "Pick up the hen and place it on the first step of the stairs."

"If I am to do this, Lord, stop the hen from cackling", she prayed. Think of a hen laying an egg and not being able to cackle! There was an old box on top of the stairs, and into the box the hen went. She didn't cackle and she did lay an egg! That hen came every day until one day the doctor said she should change her diet and that was the day the hen

Faith

on the doorstep was frightened and never returned. Faith had provided the humble maid with eggs as long as she needed them.

Oh, to believe and see God provide, to see the God who sent the ravens to Elijah with food, working for us! God give us this gift of faith. All things are possible to him that believeth!

—5—

Gifts of Healing

Let us turn for our reading to 1 Corinthians 14:1-6, and then to 12:9: "To another faith by the same Spirit; to another the gifts of healing by the same Spirit."

This evening we are going to consider gifts of healing. God delights to heal His people. During the forty years that the children of Israel were marching across the desert, there was not one feeble person in all their tribes. God can keep us all well; isn't that a pleasant thought! We can be well and strong in the Lord!

Gifts of healing—notice, please, that it is a composite gift; it does not say "gift" of healing, but "gifts." Although it is one manifestation, it is a composite manifestation, even as a bunch of grapes is not one grape, but a cluster of many grapes; so with gifts of healing, there are many gifts all clustered together in the one composite manifestation.

One might ask, "How many gifts are there?" Where the Bible is silent it is a very good thing to remain silent, and not to speak when the Bible doesn't speak, or to speak only as far as the Bible does. I will go only as far as I find light in God's Word. How many

Gifts of Healing

gifts, we are asked, are there in this manifestation?

In the New Jerusalem there will be the tree of life, and it says that on the tree of life there are twelve different kinds of fruit. Every fruit will have its own leaf, so there will be twelve different kinds of leaves. It says that the leaves of the tree are for the healing of the nations; so it may be there are twelve gifts of healing; such is my inference. Why twelve? Because it would be possible to classify all the diseases to which human nature is heir under twelve headings, in twelve categories; and if that is so, then God has covered every category of disease.

There are, we state, possibly twelve gifts—I do not positively say there are twelve, but I do know there is no disease, no infirmity, no complaint from which we suffer that God is not able to heal. Why should He give gifts of healing and not a single gift? It is possible that one person may be used more specifically in one direction than in another; in fact, we have found this to be the case.

Smith Wigglesworth was particularly interested in people who had internal trouble, such as appendicitis or colic or some internal disorder, and was greatly used of God in praying for such people. He often was a little vigorous when he prayed—he would give the sick a good shaking sometimes—but he had remarkable faith in praying for people afflicted in this way.

Some servants of the Lord are used of God in opening blind eyes, and some have a ministry particularly with goiters, growths, and cancers; not that they are not used in other ways, but more particularly in one line than another.

Now, the gifts of healing must not be confused

with healings wrought through the medical profession. The doctor doesn't heal by gifts of healing; his gift may be said to come from God (we have nothing but what the Almighty has given us), but the medical man heals according to his ability, arising out of his study of medical science. There are those who believe in the power of mind over matter; their healings are according to their power to control matter by their minds; but we do not classify such as divine healings or as coming within the category of spiritual gifts.

We do not doubt that some people, by a great concentration of mind and thought, have been able to effect remarkable results; but since unconverted people can do that, it cannot be regarded as an operation of the Holy Spirit.

Gifts of healing are manifestations of the Spirit of God. You will remember that when the prophet of the Lord was sent to Bethel a miracle took place when he cried against the altar; it split into two parts and the fire spilled out. The king, Jeroboam (who caused Israel to sin), reached forth his hand and said, "Lay hold of that man," and then found he couldn't draw his arm back again; he had been paralyzed in a moment. He turned to the man of God for help—to the one he was going to arrest and punish—to him he had to turn in humiliation and ask for prayer. The man of God prayed and that withered arm was healed in a moment.

Gifts of healing are manifestations of the power of God in the sphere of disease.

Isaiah, for instance, prayed for Hezekiah, who had been told he was going to die, and he laid a poultice of figs upon the boil. Some have supposed that the use of figs would suggest the use of means in con-

Gifts of Healing

nection with divine healing; that we should, perhaps, use a poultice, or a plaster, or some such thing on the authority of Hezekiah's experience. There are times when some external application will assist faith. I don't think there was any virtue in the figs themselves to heal the boil; figs are usually more beneficial when taken internally, but here a poultice was put on the boil and the king recovered.

It seems as if faith at times requires some help. For instance, the Lord put clay on a blind man's eyes and healed him. I don't think there was any virtue in the clay; yet He put clay on the man's eyes and told him to go and wash in the pool of Siloam. He washed and came away seeing.

Why therefore was clay put upon the man's eyes? Well, I will make a suggestion. It may have been that the man's eye sockets were empty and that what he required was more than sight; it may have been that the Lord, the great Creator, who in the beginning made man from the dust of the earth, filled up the empty eye sockets with clay, and by His mighty power changed the clay into eyes. It may have been that when he washed, he simply washed away what was not required for the creation of the eyes, the surplus. That is only a suggestion, and it may be wrong; but we do know that sometimes the application of some small thing like clay will assist faith and help a person to believe.

It was my privilege, some years ago, to be in Canada when a brother with gifts of healing was holding meetings, and I was invited to the platform. There was a long line of people coming up for prayer, and one of the first was a woman with a baby. The baby had crossed eyes. The servant of the Lord turned the mother so that everybody could see that the baby's eyes were crossed. He said to the congregation, "God is going to heal these eyes tonight and put them straight," and when he said that I thought, "What faith!" He did not say, as we might have said, "I am going to pray for this baby and ask the Lord to put its little eyes straight." He turned to the baby and prayed. How long did he pray? Did he wrestle with God? No. He may have prayed for five seconds, and then he touched the baby and turned it to the congregation. What a thrill went through the whole congregation; they shouted for joy; the work was done! He didn't even touch the baby's eyes; he touched its head, gently put his hand on the baby's head, and the eyes were made straight.

Then a man came who was deaf and dumb; His mother brought him. He was six feet tall. The preacher asked, "What is the matter with him?" His mother said, "He is deaf and dumb." The preacher said to the people, "This man is deaf and dumb; the Lord is going to heal him." I thought, "O man, great is thy faith." Now, the preacher was not very tall, and he had to reach his hand up high to pray for this man. This time he prayed approximately ten seconds.

Then he said to the man, "Can you hear me?" and the man answered, "Yes." The evangelist went to one side and said, "Can you hear me?" and the man said, "Yes." He went to the back of the man: "Can you hear me?" "Yes." I should have liked to hear the man say more than "Yes," but he didn't; he said "Yes" every time he was spoken to. The preacher said to the mother, "Now, you see he can hear and speak; teach him some words," and they went off the platform rejoicing.

Gifts of Healing

These remarkable instances of healing stimulate faith. With God all things are possible, and supernatural healings show that God is in the midst of His people.

Now, talking of healing generally, let us note first of all that we are to pray for ourselves: "Is any among you afflicted? let him pray" (James 5:13) and that affliction means sickness. If we are sick, the first thing to do is to pray for ourselves, not to run to someone else and ask, "Please pray for me."

It goes on to say, "Pray one for another, that ye may be healed." Now, that's a united effort in prayer. But first it says, "Is any sick among you? let him call for the elders of the church; and let them pray over him, anointing him with oil in the name of the Lord: and the prayer of faith shall save the sick, and the Lord shall raise him up; and if he has committed sins, they shall be forgiven him" (James 5:14, 15).

Note, "the Lord shall raise him up,"—that is, when you are sick in bed and you cannot get up, you can call for the elders; and if they are godly men and fervent in praying, they will pray for you, and the Lord, in response to the prayers of these godly men, will raise you up; and if you have committed sins, which perhaps have been the cause of the sickness, then the Lord will forgive your sins as He heals your body.

But in addition to these healings, there are gifts of healing in the Church, and gifts of healing are amazing.

Think of Elisha and Naaman. Naaman the Syrian, the enemy of the Lord, the enemy of Israel, had made raids on Israel and had slain God's people, and had taken some of them captive. He had a girl in his home who was a captive from Israel, and the little girl talked about the great prophet in her country, and said to her mistress, "I am sure that the prophet in my country could heal my master of his leprosy," and the woman told her husband. A dying man will clutch at a straw, and a leper is ready to hear of any possibility of healing; so he obtained letters from the King of Syria and went to the King of Israel to get healed. What a mistake! What do kings know about divine healing?

The King of Israel rent his clothes and said, "This is intrigue; he has not come to me to get healed; he has come to spy out the land and there will be another raid soon." The prophet heard about it and said, "Let him come down to me and he shall know there is a God in Israel."

So Naaman went down to the prophet's house, doubtless full of ideas of what would take place. He would possibly say to himself, "I know what will happen; when I come down in my chariot with my servants, the prophet will come out with a whole retinue of servants behind him; he will bring with him dragon's blood, holy fire, and a crystal; I will show him the place of the leprosy, and he will begin to mutter and mumble and chant something, and then in his rites he will smite the leprosy, and it will be instantly healed."

Doubtless he was imagining something like that, but when he came to the house the prophet didn't even show his face. Naaman didn't even see the man, and that upset his dignity. Out came a servant who said, "Go, dip in Jordan seven times and you will be healed."

That put Naaman in a rage, for he was not used

Gifts of Healing

to being treated like that; people thought it was an honor to speak to such a great general, and here is a man who does not show his face but sends out a servant. "If I want to dip anywhere I will dip in Abana and Pharpar—better rivers than this muddy Jordan," he mutters.

There was a soft-spoken person among the servants of Naaman who persuaded his master to try the cure; he got him down to the Jordan, where Naaman stripped himself, dived in, and came up—not even a tiny bit better. There is nothing in the Bible to say he was better after the first dip. The servant would say, "Sir, that is only once." So down he went the second time and came up sputtering—and I don't think he was any better the second time. But he dipped the third time, and the fourth, fifth, and sixth, complaining all the time. Then he dipped the seventh time, and at that moment the leprosy disappeared and there was new flesh in its place, like the flesh of a child. The part of Naaman which had been worst—where the leprosy was—became the best part of his body, for the flesh there was like the flesh of a little child.

And the man of God wasn't even present at the time of the healing. He sent him down to obey a word. It is when we obey the Word that the work is done. Naaman had to act, helped by his servant, on the strength of the Word. He had to go in obedience to the Word. He would have gone back home still leprous if the servont had not helped him. Even the faith he exercised was God's gift to him—it was all of God.

I suppose one of the most astonishing instances of healing that has ever happened was through the brazen serpent, when God said to Moses: "Make thee a fiery serpent, and set it upon a pole: and it shall come to pass that every one that is bitten, when he looketh upon it, shall live" (Numbers 21:8).

How can a look at a serpent on a pole cleanse the poison from the bloodstream? I don't know, but I know that it happened, because God said, "Look and live." Those who were bitten and could feel the poison going through their bodies, were healed when they turned their eyes to the serpent on the pole.

Now, that was mass healing; that was not praying for one at a time, for a hundred could look at the same moment and a hundred would be healed instantly.

I want to give you a personal experience. Some years ago I came back from travels in Japan, China, and Korea with malaria. I went home across Siberia and the malaria clung to me affectionately! I tried to leave it behind, but could not shake it off; so when I got home I went to bed. First, the ague; then the fever; and then the exhaustion, day after day.

I was chairman of the Assemblies of God Fellowship in the British Isles at the time, and when the annual conference time came, I was in bed. They said, "What is going to happen?" I said, "God must undertake for me; I can't go to the Conference with malaria." I had three hot-water bottles—one for my back, one for my feet, and one I hugged—and I still was not warm. When I did get warm I got too hot, went on to the fever, then to delirium, followed by prostration.

The meetings were to commence on a Monday, and I had been invited to take some meetings on the previous Sunday near to where the Conference would be held. On Friday I said, "Now, Lord, this must be the

Gifts of Healing

test day; if I have malaria today I shall have to write to say I cannot attend."

As I sat in a chair by the fire I felt something happening. I hoped and wondered, dared to believe, and God be thanked, I had no malaria that day.

On Saturday I traveled; on Sunday I preached; and during the week following I had three meetings a day and also extra sessions. We were busy from nine o'clock in the morning till nine-thirty at night, the entire week. People said, "I thought you had malaria," and I said, "I did up till last week."

The meetings ended on Friday, and on Saturday a friend was taking me home in his car. When he got near to London I said, "Oh, step on the gas." He said, "What is the matter?"

"Malaria!" I answered.

"Malaria?" he asked.

"Yes, as quick as you can to London."

I reached home, and crawled into bed. The hot-water bottles were there, and I was as bad as ever with malaria.

You say, "What happened?" I had enjoyed a week's exemption from the illness. I thought I was healed, but I wasn't. The Lord knew I had to take the Conference. He had given me the office as Chairman, so it was necessary to be supported in it, and for that complete week I was free.

A tour around the British Isles had been planned for me. The matron of the Bible school said, "You won't be able to go." I said, "Now don't say that; you remember what God did for me during the Conference." The malaria stopped, and I have never had it since. God is wonderful!

But I must tell you, in closing, about the woman

who was ill at Grimsby. The poor soul lay on a four-wheel stretcher. She loved to come to the meetings. She was only skin and bones, and as white as a sheet, with sunken dark eyes. She looked as if she was ready to die—about the worst case I have ever seen in a church. There she lay, and she would hold up her hand to be shaken, and you were almost afraid to shake her hand lest her fingers break. I got a pain in my stomach when I looked at her. She was always there when anyone preached, for she liked to go to the meetings; they did her good.

I said in my heart, "If God would heal this woman I would talk about it," and it was a test case! She was about as ill as a person can be—a living skeleton! So I went on my itinerary around the British Isles, and came back to Grimsby, but the stretcher was not there. That was not extraordinary, because a woman in that condition could die any minute, or be too ill to be wheeled to church.

We started the meeting and were singing the first hymn when in came a woman so vigorously that she shook the floor. I said to myself, "I know that person; I have seen her somewhere," and instead of thinking about the hymn (may the Lord forgive me) I was thinking about that woman. She had rosy cheeks, and she sang lustily.

Then it came to me; this was the woman from the stretcher! A greater miracle I have never seen, because most people when they have been ill show some evidence of it—a pallor, with dark lines under the eyes or the like. Oh, it was marvelous; this woman was totally changed. Instead of being as white as a sheet, she was rosy; and instead of being weak, she was vigorous. How did it happen?

Gifts of Healing

I learned that one day faith came into her heart, and she said to her relatives, "Take me to Stephen Jeffreys." He was holding meetings in Louth, in Lincolnshire.

They said, "You cannot go!"

"Yes, I can, I am going to be healed."

"No!"

She said, "I want to go."

They talked among themselves and said, "We know what this is; it is her dying wish and we cannot deny her; we must take her somehow. She may die on the way, or coming back, but she must go."

"And take my clothes with me," she said, and so they took her clothes. They would do anything to humor her.

They got her on the train with her four-wheel stretcher and took her to the meetings at Louth. The evangelist, Stephen Jeffreys, left the platform, came to her stretcher, and prayed as he laid his hands upon her. She said afterwards that she felt a divine hand under her spine lifting her up. She put her feet over the side of the stretcher and on to the floor. The evangelist held her as she attempted to balance. She took a few steps with his aid; then he released her, and she walked around the church; later she walked around the market square between the meetings. A crowded church witnessed this great miracle.

Jesus is alive. The gifts of the Holy Spirit are in the church today—faith can accomplish mighty things, and what we need today is more manifestation of God in our midst.

—6—

The Working of Miracles

We will take for our reading 1 Corinthians 12:27-31 and 13:1-13.

The gift that we are considering is mentioned in 1 Corinthians 12:10: "To another the working of miracles." This is a spectacular gift, full of signs and wonders; a gift that was more in evidence in the Old Testament than in the New. In the New Testament God was showing His compassion; in the Old Testament He was demonstrating His power.

Some people have erroneously supposed that the power of God is demonstrated only in the conversion of souls. It goes without saying that the conversion of a soul is a supernatural experience; it is indeed a miracle. A person does not become converted by turning over a new leaf or living a better life; he is converted when the power of God gives him new life.

The working of miracles, however, is a supernatural manifestation of the power of God that alters, suspends, or in some other way controls the laws of nature. It is a remarkable gift. Elijah had it when he parted the Jordan. He smote the waters step by step; the waters divided hither and thither; and he went over on dry land. That was a miracle.

The Working of Miracles

The Lord Jesus began His ministry with a miracle. You recall that He was invited to a wedding feast. It is nice to think that He can sanctify a wedding, and certainly a Christian wedding. The Lord joined our first parents together in the garden a long time ago. Jesus was at the wedding in Cana, and they ran short of wine. That was a sad thing, for there should not be any shortages on a wedding day. After you are married there may be a few shortages, but there should not be any on the wedding day.

Perhaps it was a hot day, or the guests were particularly thirsty; whatever the reason, they consumed the quantity provided, and Mary told Jesus they had no wine.

He must have talked faith previously in such a way that He inspired His mother to believe He could do anything—that there was nothing impossible with Him—because she said, "They have no wine." He said, "Woman, what have I to do with thee? Mine hour is not yet come" (John 2:3, 4).

Why did He not say, "Mother"? I believe He was offended in His spirit and objected to Mary's suggesting that He should work a miracle. Why? Because God Himself was the One who showed Him what to do. He said that in His ministry later. However, she prevailed upon Him.

This beginning of miracles Jesus performed in Cana of Galilee. It was by the power of the Spirit working through Him. He did not normally take orders from human beings. Mary was certainly making a mistake when she suggested that He perform a miracle. Only God has that prerogative, and so Jesus was inwardly offended; and instead of thinking of Mary as His mother, He thought of her as a woman.

It was, we may say, Deity speaking to humanity, because humanity had sought to govern Deity. We can prevail upon God and cause Him to do what He otherwise would not do. She went further and said to the servants, "Whatsoever he saith unto you, do it." He was therefore committed to action.

He said, "Fill the waterpots with water." Ah, they were to fill the waterpots, the fullness signifying how we should fulfill the commandments. They didn't partly fill the waterpots; they filled them to the brim. As they poured and the water went over the lip of the waterpot, it changed from colorless, tasteless water into purple wine, sweet and luscious.

The governor of the feast, the best man, sampled this fresh supply, and it tasted delicious. He said, "Men usually bring out the best wine first, but you have kept the best wine till the last." Jesus had done nothing of the kind—this was a new and miraculous supply. I would like to point out here that Jesus can make better wine than anybody else on earth. We cannot improve on anything Jesus does. He can produce better joy than anybody else—purer, greater joy.

Why did Jesus not want to make wine on this occasion? Because He had not come into the world to make wine for people who had drunk well, nor had He come to make bread for those who were full and satisfied. He came to make food for the hungry, and to make it superabundantly. But Jesus began His ministry with this wonderful miracle of turning water into wine. In contrast, Moses turned the water into blood and nobody could drink it. When Jesus turned the water into wine they could not drink enough of it!

The Working of Miracles

Why should God be pleased to impart the working of miracles to a person? In the first place, miracles are given as credentials. When Moses fled from Egypt and arrived in the desert of Midian, he found some shepherds driving away shepherdesses from the well, and he helped the women to water their flock. In consequence, the shepherdesses arrived home earlier than usual. Their father, Jethro, the priest of Midian, asked, "How is it that ye are come so soon today?" They replied that an Egyptian delivered them out of the hand of the shepherds and also drew water enough for them and watered the flock. He said, "Where is he? Call him that he may eat bread." They brought him home and Moses was content to dwell with the man. A romance sprang up in that home and Moses married one of the daughters.

Now he became a shepherd, and as he was minding the sheep one day a bush burned with fire without being consumed. Seeking to discover the reason for the perpetual flame, he heard the voice of God speaking to him out of the midst of the fire: "Moses, put off thy shoes from off thy feet, for the place whereon thou standest is holy. . . . I have seen the affliction of my people ... and I will send thee unto Pharaoh" (Exodus 3:5).

But Moses feared to obey. God said, "I will be with thee." Moses said, "If I go into Egypt whom shall I say has sent me?" "Say I AM hath sent thee." (For God's name is, "I am that I am." He is the almighty; He is omnipresent; He is omniscient. He brings the eternal past and the eternal future into the present.)

Moses said, "If I go into Egypt and say I AM hath sent me, they will not believe me." God said, "What is that in thine hand?" "It is a rod," he said, and he threw it down. In a moment the thing was moving—it became a serpent, and Moses fled before it. God called him back and said, "Go and pick it up," and he picked it up by the tail.

I would think that is the wrong way to pick up a snake; there are so many vertebrae in its spinal column that it can turn around without the least difficulty, and its head can touch its tail. I don't quite know what is the right way to pick up a snake, but if God told Moses to pick it up by the tail, that was the right way. He touched the tail and it became his rod again.

Then God said, "Now put your hand in your bosom." He did so and when he took it out again it was white with leprosy. He had the most dreaded disease an Easterner can have; he was a leper, as white as snow. God said, "Put it back into thy bosom." When he took it out the leprosy was gone. Then God said, "Now go into Egypt."

He went into the court of Pharaoh, one of the greatest monarchs of the day, and announced, "I AM hath sent me." Pharaoh said, "Who is I AM?"

Moses said, "I will demonstrate," and he threw down his rod in the king's palace and it turned into a serpent. Jannes and Jambres said, "Your majesty, don't be fooled by what he is doing." They had their magic wands and they turned them into serpents. Now there were three serpents wriggling in the palace.

Then a wonderful thing took place: Moses' snake swallowed the other two. When he picked up his rod again his rod was three in one.

The devil's power is mighty, but God is almighty. There are powers of the devil that are really stupendous, but God's power is over all. These were the credentials that God had sent Moses, and Pharaoh had to know that.

Sometimes the working of miracles is used as a sign. The children of Israel demanded a king that they might be like the other nations. God didn't want them to be like the nations; He wanted them to be His own peculiar people. But they insisted, and God said, "Give them a king."

Samuel said, "I will show you the greatness of your sin." It was a summer's day, and I presume the sun was shining brightly and the grain was waving in a gentle breeze. Everything seemed ready for harvest, for cutting the grain. Samuel said, "I am going to pray, and God will send a thunderstorm."

The sky turned a slate gray and there were flashes of lightning. Down came the rain, beating down the grain in the time of harvest, and it all came in a moment of time. This miracle was a sign of God's displeasure, and was an answer to Samuel's believing prayer, although prayer is not always essential to the functioning of the gift.

I want you to notice that it does not say the "gift of miracles," but the gift of the *"working* of miracles." Why are those extra words there? There are no superfluous words in the Bible. It is the *working* of miracles, and this is significant. God gives this gift to a person that he might use the power of God for His glory, demonstrating miracles so that all can see. It is not the praying for or hoping for miracles; it is the *working* of them.

You remember when Jesus was in the boat and it began to fill with water. The disciples were afraid of drowning and Jesus lay in the hinder part of the boat.

They awakened Him. They said, "Master, carest thou not that we perish?" (Mark 4:38). He rose up and rebuked the wind.

He might have prayed, O my heavenly Father, thou seest my faithful disciples afraid they are going to die. According to thy purpose and thy plan, wilt thou cause the storm to be stopped." That would be praying for a miracle, but He did not pray at all. He said, "Peace, be still," and the wind dropped and a great calm came over the sea. It was the *working* of the miracle; He worked it.

When He came to the fig tree, why did He not bless it? Because He was showing, doubtless, what is going to happen to us if we stand at the judgment with leaves of profession only and not fruits. He cursed the barren fig tree. He said, "Let no fruit grow on thee henceforward for ever" (Matthew 21:19). He did not pray, "Thou seest it is not fit to live; be pleased to destroy it." He spoke to the fig tree. One might say, "It has no ears." Jesus went so far as to talk to the dead. When they carried a man out of the gate of Nain, Jesus stopped the funeral. He said, "Young man, I say unto thee, arise," and the dead man heard His voice. He did not pray for a miracle; it was the working of it.

Let me tell you a little story. It happened years ago when I was ministering in Wales. I was preaching in a different place every night, and it was hard going. One night was spent with a miner in one of the little houses standing in a long, long line next to each other; and if any house was weak, the others on either side held it up. In this home, there were two bedrooms. I was given the better of the two, the front bedroom.

The Working of Miracles

I tried to go to sleep, but outside my window was an oil lamp. There was evidently water in the pipe, for the light went up and down, alternating continually; it would go down until it was almost negligible and then up again. This worried me. If anyone has suffered from nerves, he will understand. Anything mechanical or regular in its alternation (the room now flooded with light and then with darkness) is unbearable.

I could not sleep. What could I do? I prayed fervently, "Oh, Lord, you know how bad my nerves are; please stop that thing outside." Nothing happened in spite of all my praying.

I sat up in bed and said, "It has got to stop!" There were beads of perspiration on my brow, for I felt the thing must stop. I decided that if it is all right to talk to the wind and the waves, I could talk to the lamp. I waited until the unction of the Spirit was upon me; then I took a deep breath and cried out, "In the name of the Lord, stop!" It did! When I commanded, "In the name of the Lord," it stopped. I lay back in bed delighted, and had such a wonderful time with God. I had not been able to sleep when the flame went up and down, and now I could not sleep for sheer joy when it didn't go up and down!

I don't know how long it was before I actually did fall asleep, or how long I slept, but it was still dark when I awoke and I began another little praise service. Then something happened, as sometimes may have happened to you—the trouble returned. The light went up and down again.

People will sometimes get a remarkable healing from some horrible, malignant trouble, and it will be marvelous. They generally go about giving their testimony; then maybe nine months or a year after, the symptoms of the trouble return, and they will ask, "Brother Carter, what should I do?" I reply, "Refuse to doubt; you are healed; God's power has triumphed."

Now, let me finish the story of the lamp which again began to fluctuate. I said in a loud voice, "No, you don't! You stop!" This time it stopped, and it gave me no more trouble. If you have had the victory, keep it; don't let the devil prevail.

Moses passed his rod over Egypt, and frogs appeared in pots and pans, and in the dough—frogs all over the house and everywhere. The magicians passed their wands over and they made more frogs and added to the trouble. But mark, they could not get rid of any! They had the power to produce, but they did not have the power to remove. Not until Moses passed his rod over the land did the frogs go away. There is a limitation to demon power, but not to divine power. We could say a great deal more about this wonderful working of miracles.

When Elisha was going to build the school for the sons of the prophets, he got his students to help him. Some young men are better at theology than tree felling. One lost he ax head; he didn't know the ax head was loose. He said to Elisha, "I have lost my ax head."

Elisha didn't say, "Here is a little money to buy another one." A miracle, he assured the man, would be wrought in order to bring the ax head to the surface. Elisha got a little twig and dropped it in the river, and the iron did swim. A miracle because money was short!

Oh, the things we could see take place if only

The Working of Miracles

we believed for the working of miracles; we have not yet seen all the things God is willing to do. There is going to be a mighty demonstration of divine power when we believe God. Let us pray that these gifts will be in manifestation in the Church.

—7—

Prophecy

Now I propose to speak to you about the gift of prophecy. This is a very important gift because it is so greatly misunderstood.

The gift of prophecy is the simplest form of inspired utterance in a known language. It contains no direct revelation; it is comparable with the gift of tongues with interpretation, which likewise contains no revelation. It is important to state this because revelation is so often attributed to the gift of prophecy, and the reason for the misunderstanding is that certain Bible terms are interchangeable they can be used specifically or in a general way.

Speaking in a specific way, the gift of prophecy contains no revelation, but speaking in a general way it can include any spoken gift.

If a revelation comes through the gift of prophecy, it is not the gift of prophecy that is functioning alone, but two gifts are in manifestation. Suppose these two fingers I am holding up were two candles, and suppose there was a light at the top of each candle. I have two candles, but if I bring these candles together at the top, I have one flame; but that one flame, let us remember, comes from two sources.

Now prophecy can have revelation in it, but then there will be two gifts functioning together; there is the gift of prophecy, which is the simplest form of inspired utterance in a known language, and there is the revelation by the word of wisdom or the word of knowledge. Both are functioning together, burning as one holy flame. Because this has not been understood, people have been confused in their minds respecting prophecy.

Prophecy is a simple gift. Mary had it when the angel appeared; she said, "My soul doth magnify the Lord, and my spirit hath rejoiced in God my Saviour" (Luke 1:46, 47). We could call this lovely gift the poetry of the Spirit. King David had it; he prayed his prayers, and the Spirit of God touched him as he was on his knees, so that these prayers became psalms, and these psalms were prophecy. God has been pleased to preserve for us the prayers of David because they were prayed in the power of the Holy Spirit. I like to think of David on his knees as greater than his great son Solomon who sat on his throne and talked to men. David knelt before God and prayed, and God breathed upon him as he prayed and made his prayers prophetic.

The gift of prophecy is not what some people have supposed, merely a repetition of Scripture verses. I remember being in a meeting some years ago and a woman, who must have had a remarkable memory, began reciting Scripture verses during the prayer time. They followed one another very nicely, and it was remarkable how many Scriptures she strung together. When she finished, I said, "What was that, Sister?" She said it was prophecy. It seemed strange to me that God should be interested in quoting the King

James' version of the Bible all the time; I regarded it as a glorified form of that little book called *Daily Light*.

I do not say that Scripture verses will not come into prophecy, but I do say that God does not have to give us a gift of prophecy to produce a spiritual mosaic of verses from the Bible. Prophecy is not simply quoting Scripture verses; it is the flow of the Spirit as God gives utterance.

Some people have thought that prophecy was inspired preaching, and indeed we could do with more inspired preaching; but I think we must draw a line of demarcation between what we call inspired preaching and prophecy. Some preachers are able to let their minds and tongues flow so easily that they become remarkably eloquent when they preach; whereas, others are just ordinary and cannot rise to these sublime heights and pour out torrents of words in a passion of eloquence.

Prophecy cannot be preaching because prophecy requires no preparation—and believe me, preaching does, and plenty of it—for the Bible says, "Labor in the word and in doctrine" (1 Timothy 5:17), but it never says, "labor in the gift of prophecy." Preaching is usually rewarded with an offering but no one would think of receiving an offering for one who stood in the pulpit and prophesied! That would shock every spiritually minded person; but if you invite a man to preach and he has labored in the Word, don't send him away empty, but give him a little to console him and help him to support his wife and family. So there is a very practical difference between preaching and prophecy.

Prophecy has no power to save—nor indeed has any

of the gifts, for the gifts are signs that point to Christ, and Christ is the One who saves. We are saved, writes Paul, through the foolishness of preaching—not, of course, by foolish preaching. What would sound foolish to the Greeks, in comparison with their philosophical reasoning, was the power of God unto salvation to every one that believed. Jesus said, "The words that I speak unto you they are spirit and they are life." When we preach we are giving that Word which is spirit and life; but when we prophesy we speak under the unction of the Spirit.

In this connection, notice the events in Acts chapter two. On the Day of Pentecost, when the Church began and the disciples were baptized with the Holy Ghost, they came staggering down from the Upper Room and thousands gathered; yet nobody was saved by the speaking with tongues until Peter arose to preach. If the gifts had converting power there would have been some saved before Peter preached; but instead, what did they do? Some mocked, some doubted, some were astonished. Then Peter stood up and preached, and three thousand were saved.

Another reason I do not regard preaching as an exercise of the gift of prophecy is that you cannot invite a person to come and prophesy. No one would dream of saying, "Oh, Mr. Jones, come along to our meeting and give us a prophecy about three quarters of an hour in length." You can tell a preacher, "We haven't much time this morning; you have only twenty minutes; tonight we shall have more time and you can take thirty minutes," but you could not talk this way to one exercising the gift of prophecy.

I don't think preaching is prophesying because when we preach we use ordinary language, whereas it is not ordinary when we prophecy; there is an inspiration, a beauty of expression that is unusual. The language is not in the form in which people usually speak; it is poetic.

There is another thing about prophecy: it does not improve by practice, as preaching does. The person under the unction of the Spirit can utter a prophecy as beautiful in his first utterance as any he utters throughout his life, if there is no impediment. Why? because the gifts of the Spirit of God are perfect from their inception; there is no improvement. With natural gifts, improvement is the order of the day—they are there to be improved—but not so with the supernatural gifts of God. Of course, it is possible to have an impediment—to have the channel blocked. Some do not get into wonderful liberty at first. But I have heard a person speak in prophecy for the first time as clearly and as powerfully as anyone who has been baptized twenty years.

This gift of prophecy can convict people of sin. A sinner coming into a meeting and hearing a prophecy may fall down on his face and call on the name of the Lord; he will acknowledge that God is in you of a truth. When a man is convinced that God is in the midst, it is not hard to show him the way of salvation.

Prophecy is a lovely, simple gift containing in itself no revelation, but by it all the spoken gifts can function. Let me give you a verse to show that the gift of prophecy contains no revelation. Look at 1 Corinthians 14:6. The apostle writes, "Now, brethren, if I come unto you speaking with tongues, what shall I profit you, except I shall speak to you either by revelation, or by knowledge, or by prophesying, or by doctrine?"

Prophecy

There are two distinct contrasts here. If revelation were contained in the simple gift of prophecy, he would not have written *"revelation,* knowledge, *prophecy* or doctrine." Then we have verse three as well: "He that prophesieth speaketh unto men to edification, and exhortation, and comfort." It does not say, "to revelation." Also, let us note that when it uses the term "prophesying" it is being used in a general way and not in a specific way.

Zacharias was smitten dumb for doubting the angel's message; upon the birth of John his powers of speech returned, and he began to prophesy, and from his lips flowed that sublime utterance that is recorded in the Gospel of Luke.

We should desire spiritual gifts. This gift of prophecy, which we should covet more than to speak with tongues and interpretation, can lead on to the other gifts we desire, and we can more easily believe for the other spiritual manifestations when we have this gift.

—8—

Discerning of Spirits

Let us turn to 1 Corinthians 12, commencing with verse 27.

The gifts of the Holy Spirit are all miraculous, divinely miraculous; they bring into our midst the presence and power of God. This is what we are needing so greatly in the Church today—God in mighty manifestation! These gifts, being from the Holy Spirit, are as high above natural gifts as the heavens are high above the earth.

When a person manifests a natural talent he receives credit for it; but when the gifts of the Holy Spirit are in manifestation, God receives the glory. This makes such a difference!

I wish to speak about the gift of discerning of spirits, and also the gift of prophecy.

The discerning of spirits is a supernatural revelation of the unseen world. We cannot, with our natural eye, see a spirit; but if God gives to us this gift, then we can look beyond the veil and see into the realm of spirits. It does not imply the discerning of wicked spirits only; nor does it state the discerning of good spirits only; it must, therefore, mean both good and bad, whatever spirit God wishes to reveal.

Discerning of Spirits

Some people have supposed they possessed the discerning of spirits, and have said to me, "Brother Carter, I have the discerning of spirits, I know all the hypocrites in the church." Others will say, "I have the discerning of spirits; I can see demons."

Well, the gift is not the discerning of demons or of hypocrites alone. It might include both, but it is the discerning of all spirits, and there are good spirits as well as evil spirits.

I remember a dear lady who came to our meetings in Birmingham, who was not in favor of the Pentecostal Movement. I persuaded her to come and I hoped she would enjoy the meeting. We had a good time of blessing that night, and after the meeting I said to her, "What did you think of our gathering tonight?" "Oh," she said, "there were demons everywhere!" Well, I am glad to report that the saints of the Lord had a good time anyhow, for the Lord was mightily present. That dear soul just imagined she had the discerning of spirits.

A lot of people who think they have the gift of discerning of spirits are only hypocrite hunters. I have wondered (may I be forgiven) if, perchance, they might not discover another by looking in the mirror and they would not need the discerning of spirits to see this one.

The discerning of spirits is the power, as I have said, to look into the other world, to see the unseeable, and to have such revelation as God is pleased to give. It carries with it the power to judge, of course, for it is not sufficient to see into the other world; you must, of necessity, be able to judge what you see; otherwise you would not know a good spirit from a bad one.

We had a lady in London years ago who had the discerning of spirits. She had some wonderful visions and revelations. One day she saw a face; it was smiling at her in the vision. She looked intently at the face for she was perplexed. She said finally, "You are not my Lord." Then the smile disappeared and in a moment an awful frown, a terrible scowl came on that face. She grew afraid and said, "Oh, Lord, deliver me," and the face disappeared, and the face of the Lord came in its place.

How do we distinguish a good spirit from a bad one? This is difficult to explain, but I suppose it would be just as difficult to explain, how the lamb knows the bleat of its mother. Jesus said, "My sheep hear my voice, and I know them, and they follow me." The gift carries with it the power to judge.

Discerning of spirits enables us to see things we cannot see with the natural eye. For instance, people have seen the similitude of God Himself, as Ezekiel did. He saw the cherubim and the throne, and he saw the similitude of God on the throne in that first magnificent vision that he received by the river Chebar.

Then some people have seen the Lord Jesus exalted, as did Stephen when he was in the council and looked up. He was not looking at the ceiling, but beyond it, and by the power of the Spirit saw Jesus standing at the right hand of God in heaven.

Many have seen angels. Jacob saw a vision of angels and was much encouraged and cheered by the vision. Zacharias saw an angel of the Lord standing beside the altar.

Some people have seen the devil. Evil spirits have

Discerning of Spirits

been seen, as Micaiah saw the evil spirits that were going to tempt and overthrow Ahab.

Years ago, at a time when I was seeking for the baptism of the Holy Spirit, we were at the town of Bedford. A number of us young men were sleeping in a tent, our feet to the pole. There we lay like the spokes of a wheel, lying flat on the earth. In the daytime we attended a conference. One night, one wonderful night, I awoke. Everyone else was fast asleep; I could see and hear them. A holy light was filling the place; it was wonderful. I said to myself, "The moon is shining." No! There was no moon, it was a glory light. I was thrilled and said to myself, "What shall I do? Shall I awake the others?" It was one of the times in my life when I felt a strong restraint; I wanted to waken them all that they might share the glory, but, for some reason I cannot explain, I was not permitted to do so, and there I was for some moments in the glory. I said, "Speak, Lord, for thy servant heareth," but I heard no voice. That is the only vision I have ever had, small as it is, and since that day the glory of God has always been a fascinating subject with me.

But let me refer to a case in the Bible. Elisha in Dothan was surrounded by the Syrian army. They intended to capture Elisha, who had been revealing to Israel's king the secret plans of the king of Syria. They surrounded the city of Dothan and the prophet found himself in a dilemma; but a dilemma for such a one as Elisha would not be quite the same as for us, since he expected God to work, and work mightily. Elisha's servant was afraid. "Oh, master, what shall we do?" Elisha prayed, "Lord, open the young man's eyes; let him see the unseeable; let him know by holy vision something of the mighty power of God that is with us; for more are those with us than those who are against us." The Lord opened the young man's eyes, giving him the discerning of spirits, and he saw the hill full of the chariots of the Lord. He was not afraid anymore. So the discerning of spirits can be very comforting, and sometimes quite amazing.

When Stephen Jeffreys, a former coal miner, was beginning his remarkable ministry in South Wales, his church was packed to the doors with a revival service every night of the week and all day Sunday.

One night in 1914 as he was preaching the people were not looking intently at the preacher as they generally did, but were looking behind him at the wall. He was curious to know why everybody had turned their gaze, so he turned to look and there upon the wall was a likeness of the head of a lamb. Oh, he could not preach anymore! As they all watched, the vision changed into the head of the Man of Sorrows, and people began to weep, while some cried for mercy. This was not the discerning of spirits for one person; it was an enlargement, as it were, of the gift, the same as you can have an enlargement of the gifts of healing such as the time of which it is written, "The power of the Lord was present to heal." (I have been in a meeting where the power of God was present to heal; people who had no gifts of healing were believing to lay hands on people and see them healed during that time while the Lord's healing power was present.)

Here was a manifestation of this gift of discerning—or rather an enlargement of the gift—and everybody could see this wonderful vision of the head of the Man of Sorrows. People ran home to tell their rel-

Discerning of Spirits

atives and friends, and they came in; hundreds and hundreds of people came to see the vision; they formed a line up one aisle, crossed the platform, and walked down the other aisle. They kept on coming hour after hour.

There was one man, however, who said, "I don't believe it; this is not a vision at all. I will tell you what they have done: they have a lantern concealed somewhere and they are shining it on the wall. I will prove it; I will go to the platform and pass my hand over the vision and you will see the vision come on the back of my hand." So he came up with the others and he passed his hand over the vision. Nothing appeared on the back of his hand, and he fell on his knees and cried for mercy.

It went on into the early hours of the morning; thousands of people saw that vision in the Mission Hall at Llanelly. It was a sign, the people believed; for two weeks later World War I commenced.

The discerning of spirits may operate in choosing workers for the work of God. It is desirable that we have good men for responsible positions; and who knows the heart of man and the spirit of man like the Spirit of the Lord? If He will reveal such to His people, they can choose good persons for the work of God.

Of course, the same gift that can discern the good people can see the bad. Jesus said, "Have I not chosen twelve, and one of you is demon possessed?" So Jesus knew the good and the bad. He knew Nathaniel, for when he was coming to Him, He said, "Behold an Israelite indeed, in whom there is no guile." He was seeing not just the exterior; He did not judge from his pleasant face; He was looking deeper, right into his heart. He discerned his spirit, a pure guileless spirit!

Now the discerning of spirits, I said, will include all visions, for a vision is nothing more or less than seeing the unseeable. Not everyone is visionary. I am not. I have told you of the only vision I have seen, but my mother had several, and one was a very wonderful vision. She used to pray that she might see the Lord. One stormy night—when the winds were whistling and howling outside and coming through the cracks of the window, making the venetian blinds rattle—she was sitting up in bed, unable to sleep and praying her usual prayer which she had prayed so often: "O Lord, grant that I might have a vision of Thee." Suddenly, there He stood, beyond the brass rail of the old-fashioned bedstead. He was looking away into the distance with a look of sorrow on His face, and she exclaimed, "Oh, Lord!" and He vanished away. Now she was happy, delighted that the Lord had appeared to her.

As she was rejoicing, He appeared again. This time He came near and was not looking into the distance; He was looking right into her eyes and said, "Fear not." She said, "I am not afraid, Lord," and she began to speak to Him in other tongues.

I asked, "What did He look like?" and she said, "His hair was as black as a raven, and His eyes were dark. There was a suggestion of a smile on His face, and again He vanished away." Oh, she was doubly happy. As she was rejoicing, a corner of the room blazed with light; so bright and overpowering was the light that she grew afraid and said, "Oh, Lord, I cannot see anything; art Thou there?" and she shielded her eyes with her hand. In the course of time her eyes grew accustomed to that blazing light, and in the midst of it she saw a form. His hair was white as wool; He was clothed right down to His feet; His eyes flashed like fire, and on His head was a royal diadem.

She had witnessed a threefold vision of the Redeemer. She had seen the One who went to the cross, the Man of Sorrows who bore the sins of the world; then she had seen the One who said, "I will never leave thee," the Companion on life's way; and she also had seen the exalted and glorified Lord crowned with a diadem.

—9—

Tongues and Interpretations

The Day of Pentecost began with a magnificent manifestation of the Spirit of God. There was a sound from heaven as of a mighty rushing wind, and it filled all the house where they were sitting. The Day of Pentecost is the pattern for the Church today. We want manifestations of the Spirit of God—manifestations that come from heaven. On the Day of Pentecost, all those gathered in the Upper Room at Jerusalem were filled with the Holy Spirit and began to speak with other tongues as the Spirit gave them utterance. Thus, the pattern for the Church is the speaking with other tongues as the evidence of the baptism of the Holy Spirit.

Some people contest this point and say it is not necessary to speak with other tongues. They further affirm, and with this part we must agree, that there is no specific passage of Scripture stating that all must speak in tongues when filled with the Holy Spirit. It is very significant, however, that when the Spirit was poured out on the Day of Pentecost, everyone in the Upper Room spoke with other tongues; not some of them, not half of them while the other half had other gifts instead; but they were all filled and they all began to speak with other tongues. It does not seem satisfactory, therefore, for one today to have an experience that does not precisely correspond with what they had in the Upper Room.

The speaking with other tongues, we affirm, has been given as an evidence that one is filled; for we are expected, according to the New Testament, to be able to answer a specific question, and to answer it intelligently. The question is: "Did you receive the Holy Spirit when you believed?" It is a question that must be answered. We know when we believed; we know that believing upon the Lord Jesus Christ gave us the new birth; but can we answer the question, "Have we received the Holy Spirit since we believed?" or, "Did we receive the Holy Spirit when we believed?"

We must of necessity have some specific experience that will enable us to answer this question simply and clearly. So, God has been pleased to give to us the supernatural speaking with other tongues. He it was who placed the supernatural in the Church, for the Church of Jesus Christ is essentially supernatural; it is a divinely supernatural community.

When the children of Israel came out of Egypt under Moses, God was in their midst; for He led them forth by the pillar of cloud, which at night became a pillar of fire. This, in itself, is quite significant because Israel, having that light from the pillar of fire, was never entirely in the dark. However dark the night was, the shimmering rays of that holy light were constantly over the whole encampment. If one had said to a member of that camp, "How do you know that God is in the midst of you?" he would have pointed to the pillar of cloud and said, "There is the evidence, for God is in that pillar of cloud."

Well, the Church today is not in any one place, far from it; the Church of Jesus Christ is scattered all over the world. Therefore it would not be possible for us to gather around a pillar of cloud; and since God intends the supernatural to be in His Church in constant manifestation, He has put the supernatural upon our very tongues. He has caused us to speak as the Spirit gives us utterance; so that everybody, wherever he is, may have an evidence of the supernatural upon his very tongue; and it is interesting that God should have been pleased to put the supernatural upon that unruly member of the human body.

Let us for a little while consider the speaking with tongues. People have said, "Oh, the speaking in tongues is the least of the nine gifts." Let us for a moment subscribe to that; let us accept the statement that the speaking with other tongues is the least of all the gifts. Now we will give due consideration to this least gift, since it is amazingly supernatural. A person by the power of the Spirit of God speaks in a language he has never learned; he uses a vocabulary that he has not committed to memory; he speaks clearly, not hesitantly, but fluently and positively. He speaks grammatically. It is a very remarkable thing that he should utter, by the power of the Spirit of God, a language strictly according to its grammatical construction, without knowing anything whatever about the grammar of the language.

Think of that! He speaks clearly; he speaks fluently; he speaks grammatically correct in a language he has not learned; and if that isn't enough, we may go still further and mention that he speaks idiomatically, and I suppose that is the last thing we ever do in learning a language. In learning a language we labor to commit a vocabulary to memory, or at least a sufficient number of words to hold a simple conversation, and then we struggle with the grammar to get our tenses, etc., right; and the last thing that troubles us is the idiom; yet by the Spirit of God, without the least effort upon his part, the individual can speak clearly, fluently, grammatically, and idiomatically in a language he has never learned. I affirm that it is astonishing to say the least. This is what God does with everyone who speaks in other tongues.

Then one may ask, "Why is it that the entire Church of Jesus Christ has not been amazed at this stupendous miracle? Why has not the whole Church become Pentecostal?" The answer is in the Bible, Isaiah 28:11, 12, and these are the words: "With stammering lips and another tongue will he speak to this people ... yet they would not hear." There is the indictment of of Scripture against the Church that accepts the Lord Jesus as her Saviour, but does not accept the Holy Spirit's manifestation of speaking with other tongues. Mark the words, "Yet they would not hear."

So, it is God who is speaking through the Spirit-filled person in other tongues. It is the Almighty, by the Holy Ghost, who is giving him the amazing power to articulate in a language he has never learned. Yet there are some people who love the Lord Jesus Christ but have no time for this manifestation of the Holy Spirit. It is a great pity but we must leave the matter.

Let us for a moment consider the evidence of speaking with other tongues; for the Scripture says, "Do all speak with tongues?" and the answer must of necessity be in the negative. Not everyone in the Church will speak in tongues as a public ministry; indeed, very few so speak in the church publicly; but everybody should speak in tongues to himself and to God. On the Day of Pentecost they all spoke with other tongues; and if we are to carry about with us the evidence of the baptism of the Holy Spirit, then we must continue to speak with tongues in prayer; every one of us should possess the gift and exercise it.

It is the evidence of the filling with the Spirit, exactly as it is our custom to give a lady a wedding ring—and we husbands always hope that our wives will not lose this evidence of marriage given them on the day of our betrothal. The wife carries the evidence with her, which is very good, for if any eyes go wandering about which ought not, that ring can settle the matter.

The baptism of the Holy Spirit, I say, is *evidenced* by speaking with other tongues. The evidence, however, should not be confused with the *gift*. The gift is a *public* ministry by which one can utter a message in an assembly, and another person, through the gift of interpretation, can give the meaning. He that speaks *privately* in an unknown tongue, as evidence of the Baptism, speaks not unto men but unto God. Let us deal with this more fully.

The purpose of speaking with other tongues is, firstly, to commune with God, and I want to point out that this is very important. The speaking with other tongues is the only manifestation of the Spirit that has a direct aspect of worship. It could not be said of any other gift that it is "Not unto men, but unto God." How absurd it would be to say that he that heals the sick, heals not unto men but unto God. He heals the sick for the benefit of man; it is not unto God in any sense except that healing the sick, by the power of the Spirit, brings glory to God. The

Tongues and Interpretations

speaking with other tongues as the initial evidence of the Baptism has this wonderful aspect of worship, and the apostle Paul said, "I will pray with the Spirit, and I will pray with the understanding also" (1 Corinthians 14:15). So, there are two ways to pray—with the Spirit and with the understanding also.

I shall never forget when my dear mother, years ago, received the baptism of the Holy Spirit. She received very quietly at first, but oh, what a flood of blessing! For a day or two she had difficulty in speaking her own language. She got on a streetcar and tried to ask for a ticket. To her embarrassment and the conductor's, she could not speak in her own tongue! He said, "What did you say, ma'am?" She was speaking in other tongues. She had a wonderful filling, and after that her prayer life seemed to change. She had been a devout member of the Church of England, had attended the church regularly, and had taken with her a little prayer book—a very precious little book neatly bound in leather, with lovely gilt edges. This prayer book was brought out once a week; for six days it rested, and on the Lord's Day it went to church (like some people). She would open it very reverently and read from it the same words, week after week, or follow the minister as he read his book. When she received the baptism of the Holy Spirit that little prayer book was no longer required. She would go to her room and pray for hours at a time; when we boys came into the home, we would ask, "Where is Mother?" "Upstairs praying," was the usual reply. Oh, the hours she spent communing with God! She would have had sore eyes if she had been reading out of that prayer book for so long (quite apart from the monotony of it) but now she had the Spirit of God upon her and words flowed out, both in her own language and in the language of the Spirit of God, worshiping the Lord. It is a wonderful gift, the ability to speak with other tongues; and the fact that it is miraculous I personally have abundant evidence to confirm.

Permit a little personal experience. I was born with an impediment in my speech. I didn't stutter, but I had difficulty in articulating. Try as I would, I found it difficult to articulate the consonant "R." My father had the same impediment (he took it to the grave, which I thought was taking it too far!). I wanted to get rid of this impediment, this inability to articulate, because it made me a laughingstock. If I would go into a shop, for instance, to purchase something, after the shopkeeper had asked me two or three times what I wanted, he would turn to another customer and ask, "What is he saying?" Boys laughed at me—very rudely, of course. I wanted to be a minister of Jesus Christ, but I was perplexed about this inability to pronounce the letter "R." Try as I would, I couldn't say that letter.

But during this time that I was suffering from the impediment, I received the baptism of the Holy Ghost. Then what? God gave me a language with the "R" in it, and I could say it as easily as a Scotsman! I would find myself pronouncing the "R" freely, and I would stop to listen—and then I couldn't pronounce it when I spoke in English. I would resume speaking with tongues using the "R" and then I would stop, but I could not naturally pronounce the "R." Then I did something—and here I am confiding in you—I decided to try to make it pass over from the spiritual to the natural. As I was speaking with other tongues, using

Tongues and Interpretations

the "R," immediately after using it in other tongues I would stop and attempt to say a word in English with the "R" in it. Did it pass over? It didn't, and may God forgive me for trying. It would not pass over! So if anybody knows the supernatural aspect of speaking with other tongues, it is I.

You say, "Well, how did you overcome your impediment?" After being prayed for by everybody of note, and still not being healed, I decided by the help of God to roll away the stone myself: in order to accomplish the feat, I read the Bible through from Genesis to Revelation aloud, slowly, articulating to the best of my ability, and preceding the morning reading with severe exercises that I had written myself, in order to combat the difficulty.

This speaking in tongues is wonderful, but of course it can come from another origin than the Holy Spirit. In our church in Birmingham, a man came to one of our week-night meetings who, I thought, was a visiting brother from another Pentecostal assembly in the town. I greeted him and he sat down with us, and when we got down to prayer he began speaking with tongues. When he did so, everybody in the meeting pleaded the Blood. There couldn't have been more concern if a wolf had barked in the midst of the sheep cote. I said, "Let us get up, friends," and I went straight to the man and asked him, "Do you believe in God?" He answered, "Yes." I said, "Do you believe in Christ?" He answered, "I do." I said, "Do you believe that He died for you on the cross of Calvary, and that His blood cleanses from sin?" He said, "I used to." I said, "You are possessed with the devil, and I will cast it out." Well, he did not give me the opportunity, for he made for the door as quickly as he could, and I never saw him again.

I learned from this experience that the people of God are sensitive to the Spirit; and if a demon-possessed person speaks in tongues in our meeting, we discern demon power from Holy Ghost power as easily as a little lamb knows the bleat of its mother from the bark of a wolf. Of course, there are powers that are demoniacal, but there also seem to be powers that are on the natural plane, neither demoniacal nor divine. I had a friend who had a gift of telepathy; he often could read another person's thoughts. He did not do it by the power of God, and as he was a good Christian man, he evidently did not do it by any satanic power. We do well to seek for the origin of the power and see whether it is from God, which is the only power that is of any lasting value.

Regarding the speaking in tongues, let me tell you a little story of what happened in our church in London some years ago. I was praying with the sick, and among them was a Welshman. I said to the Welshman, "What do you want from the Lord?" He said, "Hearing." I laid my hands on him and prayed, and said, "Brother, can you hear?" He put his hand around his ear and said, "What did you say?" There are some embarrassing moments in the ministry, as we have all found, and I stepped away. In that church there was a little alcove and I stepped in there and said privately, "Lord, where is the power to lay hands upon the sick that we talk about?" The power of the Spirit came upon me, and I felt it tingling through me. I went straightway to him, laid my hands on him, and God opened his ears. I was speaking with other tongues at the time, and later he gave his testimony. He said, "When

Tongues and Interpretations

God opened my ears [and he could now hear a watch ticking] Brother Carter spoke in Welsh." I want to explain that the Welsh language is very difficult for an Englishman to speak; but under the power of the Spirit I spoke to a Welshman in his own language at the moment God opened his ears.

The speaking with other tongues edifies the one who speaks: "Wherefore let him that speaketh in an unknown tongue pray that he may interpret" (1 Corinthians 14:13). He that speaks in an unknown tongue edifies himself, not with an intellectual edification, but with a building up of his spirit. There is something assuring, something strengthening to his spiritual nature that comes as a result of speaking in other tongues.

In 1914 I was in a convention in England. Alexander Boddy was the chairman and there were numerous speakers on the platform. There were several from Germany, some from Holland, and others from America, including a missionary named Miss Alma Doering. There were also a number of English speakers, including Smith Wigglesworth. Behind me in the congregation, a Scotsman spoke in other tongues; it was a clear resounding message. Mrs. Crisp, the lady principal of the Women's Bible School in London, was sitting in the front row and she gave the interpretation. The Scotsman spoke again in this tongue, and Mrs. Crisp interpreted a second time. It happened a third time. Then Miss Alma Doering, the American missionary from Africa, spoke to the chairman, and he said, "Miss Alma Doering wishes to address the Convention respecting the message that has just been given." We were all very much interested to hear what she had to say. She said: "Friends, the language that has just been spoken is the language of the Kifiote tribe in

Africa; it is next to the tribe of people among whom I am working. Just as one native will call aloud to a native on another hill, and get his attention, and then give him a message, so the Lord has spoken through the message and called us to attention, and given us the word that He would have us receive.

"Regarding the interpretation," she continued, "the sister who interpreted has given us a faithful interpretation of the message." She said, "If I had sat down with pen and paper and had translated what I heard, I should have put it in plain language; but the lady who interpreted has not only given us the sense of the message, she has given it to us in the most ornate language; it has been most beautifully expressed."

So there was a double miracle—a Scotsman who knew only English was speaking clearly and fluently in the language of the Kifiote tribe. A lady who did not even know what language it was, gave a most wonderful interpretation by the Spirit. So you see, God is doing a most amazing thing in the midst of His people.

Let me add just a little about the gift of interpretation. People have wondered about it. They have asked me, "Brother Carter, how does the gift of interpretation come?" Well, I will give a personal experience. When I first began to interpret I saw everything in the most graphic way; the Lord was pleased to give me a picture, and all I had to do was to describe it in the Spirit. Then that passed away, and I had interpretation by words. Words would come and I would just speak them out. Later came the most difficult time of all, which I am experiencing at the present time. When a message in tongues is ended

Tongues and Interpretations

I generally have nothing in my mind at all; I have to step out in the dark, as it were; or, to use a Bible figure, I have to start out in faith like Abraham, not knowing whither I am going. This gift of interpretation is a complementary gift to the speaking with other tongues. Without it a person should not speak publicly in tongues, if there is no interpreter present. He may speak once, but if no interpretation is given he should not speak a second time. Better still, let him pray that he might interpret the message himself.

Interpretations should not be given in a strained way. I knew a young man who used to twist and struggle greatly before he gave an interpretation; it seemed to be a painful experience for him.

The same thing happened in my church in London. There was a lady who had a good gift of intepretation, so we left the ministry of interpretation to her. However, she developed an idiosyncrasy that was very distressing. Members of the congregation asked me if I would speak to her about it. They were distressed about the scream that usually preceded the interpretation. I said to the sister one day, "Just come with me for one moment," and I took her away from the congregation so that I could talk with her privately. I said, "I want to speak to you about your gift of interpretation." She froze stiff, anticipating what was coming—and that didn't help me, because I always found it difficult to say anything along the line of correction to a lady. But I had to go through with it, even though the atmosphere was so antagonistic. I thought: "How can I tell her about this scream without offending her?" Then a happy thought came. I said, "Sister, what I want to say can be expressed very briefly. It is this: we want the train to start without the whistle blowing."

It was the shriek of the whistle that got on our nerves. For about three weeks after this we had no interpretations. Then the dear sister got over it and began to interpret again, and there was no struggle, no scream, but beautiful interpretations—the train without the whistle.

It is wonderful to have a message in tongues with interpretation—not that all messages are striking and remarkable, but the fact that God is in manifestation in the Church is so encouraging. It is an assurance to us that we are in the line of His will, and that we have no need to write *Ichabod* over our meetings. I trust that we shall never lose the manifestations of the Spirit of God from our Pentecostal churches.